SWIM,

RIDE,

RUN,

BREATHE

SWIM
RIDE
RUN
BREATHE

*How I Lost
a Triathlon
and Caught
My Breath*

JENNIFER GARRISON BROWNELL

THE PILGRIM PRESS
CLEVELAND

*September 2015 —
Dear Molli,
Breathe on!
with gratitude
for your many
gifts —
Jenny Brownell*

for Jeff

The Pilgrim Press, 700 Prospect Avenue, Cleveland, Ohio 44115
thepilgrimpress.com
© 2015 by Jennifer Garrison Brownell

Printed in the United States of America on acid-free paper

19   18   17   16   15   5   4   3   2   1

ISBN 978-0-8298-2023-2

CONTENTS

CONTENTS

ACKNOWLEDGMENTS

Thanks to Tina Villa, who said yes;

to Seattle University's School of Theology and Ministry, where I took the most important tests of all;

to Mary Nilsen and Melissa Wiginton, who encouraged some of these words, and to Revgalblogpals, who encouraged others of them and so much more;

to the Lilly Foundation, which funded the sabbatical;

to *Geez* magazine, which published an early draft of chapter 15;

to the good people of Hillsdale Community Church—UCC in Portland, Oregon, especially Dennis Frengle, who suggested I make a goal at the very beginning, and Cathy Thomas and Cheryl Carbone, who checked the manuscript at the very end;

to Mom, Dad, Mark, Noah, and Jacob for letting me tell a lot of stories and a few secrets;

to those whose care makes everything possible—niece-on-call Alyssa Brownell, god-family JJ, Steve, Charlotte, and Atticus, and Right at Home (especially Marlene, Lauren, Rock, Kate, Hanna, Amanda, and Reagan);

and to Jen Violi (www.jenvioli.com), book coach extraordinaire, who midwifed these words into light and life.

And most especially to Jeff and Elijah, who made room in their lives for me to train for a triathlon and room at our dining room table for this book to get written.

INTRODUCTION

I'm not like you, gym rat. I'm not even like you, moderately in-shape rat.

I'm more like you. Yes, you, over in the corner with your nose in a book. I'm the uncoordinated, voracious reader with too many knees and elbows and not enough guts. I'm the one picked last for every team, every time. I know, I know. Everyone says that, and it's not possible for *everyone* to be last but, really, I insist that I am. The last.

The story I want to tell you goes like this: I never did a single athletic thing in my life. I know, I know. Everyone says that, too. But that sentence has ellipses at the end and is usually followed by ". . . since I was on dance line" or ". . . since I ran track in middle school" or ". . . since I climbed Mt. Kombatabrutius." My sentence ends with a full stop. I never did a single athletic thing in my life. Period.

Until today. Today I'm hanging around a pool waiting for the whistle that means the sprint triathlon will be starting. Will this be it? I've been training for a while and still don't feel much like an athlete, but I'm wondering if this will be the day that I stop being whatever I was before and start being what Samuel Johnson in his wisdom called "strong of body, vigorous, lusty, robust."[1]

Me, sitting here on the edge of a pool getting ready to start a sprint triathlon. This did not begin today. It started last year, during a conversation with a stranger, a woman who was both heavier and older than I am, who said, "In the triathlon, the only thing was, I didn't want to be the fattest and I didn't want to be the slowest, and I wasn't either." And why this particular pool, this particular triathlon? That started with that conversation, too.

"What triathlon was it, the one where you were not the oldest?" I asked, innocently, as if I were just making conversation and not gathering vital information.

"It's in McMinnville?" she replied with that lift at the end that turns a statement into a question.

So maybe my triathlon started when I went home and looked it up online. The McMinnville Oregon Parks and Rec Sprint Triathlon promised a "relaxed" race that would accommodate all levels and be welcoming to beginners. It was in May, months and months away. It would be warm and, possibly (although this *is* Oregon), not raining by then. And it was a sprint triathlon, the baby of all triathlons with the shortest distances. I think of those distances in miles rather than kilometers and I round down because then it seems even shorter—swim half a mile, bike about twelve miles, run about three miles. I read the reassuring words and looked at the numbers. I wondered if maybe I could do it.

Or maybe my triathlon started a couple of months later in a conversation with a man from church about his experience being a triathlon transition assistant for his son. The conversation morphed from a story about that event into a pep talk about setting goals. "You gotta set a goal," he said.

---

1. Johnson's famous dictionary was published in 1755, after eight years of effort and with the help of at least six assistants. See, I told you. More bookworm than gym rat.

I'm not much more of a goal-setter than I am an athlete. Wait, let me put that in the past: I wasn't much more of a goal-setter than I was an athlete. That day, I set a goal.

Are you still with me, gym rat? Because *your* environment has become *mine* now. My environment used to be gently lit, quiet places with worn carpeting and the enticing scent of old books. Libraries and churches—those were my buildings. The librarian never had to shush me. She smiled over her glasses as she pressed her stamp onto an inkpad and then gently onto the card she slipped into the back of the book.

And I always liked being in churches. When I was ten, I was an acolyte, a role that came with few actual duties that I remember. Mostly I remember sitting with my friend Amy in these big thrones someone had stuck in the back of the church. The adults were preoccupied, their backs to us, so as long as we weren't too disruptive, they didn't care what we did. We laughed silently, passed notes, whispered little gossips, confident in that sweet spot between perfect safety and perfect freedom. My pastor dad's voice speaking and my mom's voice singing provided a familiar and comfortable soundtrack.

The school in our little town didn't really have a gymnasium. Instead it had a basement with a floor painted gray and a gym teacher who visited once a week from a bigger school. On days the gym teacher wasn't there, our regular teacher took us out into the yard. Then, gymnasium time was listening to a record with a song that teased us about our chicken fat while we bony pre-adolescents performed humiliating exercises such as touching our toes ten times. The word "gymnasium" comes from a Greek word meaning "to exercise naked." Of course we had clothes on, but in that little schoolyard gymnasium, I sure understood exactly what it was like to exercise naked.

In my imagination, I'm no longer naked in the schoolyard. In my imagination, I'm standing at the door of a real gymnasium, a building. In my imagination, I'm sweeping through the front doors with full confidence that I actually belong here. In my imagination, you are following me, and this is what we see.

When we get in the front door, we follow the intoxicating smell of chlorine. We'll have to walk through a slightly moldy plastic sheet cut into strips, around a corner, and down a long corridor to the locker room. Don't breathe too deeply here. The chlorine smell can't quite cover the musty too-many-wet-clothes smell. Walk through the shower and rinse off as the sign instructs. Don't look too closely at what has gathered in the drains since the last time—1997?—they were cleaned. Keep walking through the warm damp until we are beside the swimming pool. And then, look! That's me! In the pool! And I'm swimming!

I wasn't always moving even when I was in the water. There was that one day, a few months into training for the tri, when I was in the pool and wearing a swimsuit, but I was stopped. And sobbing. This was probably not what Debra (who actually calls herself an athlete and has the rugby chops to prove it) had in mind when she agreed to give me a swim lesson. I'd been teaching myself how to swim by lurking around the local community center, spying on real swimmers underwater through big Italian triathlete goggles. After months of practicing what I learned by this method, I still got out of breath with every lap. Deb said that she'd help me figure out why.

She watched me swim one length and, as usual, I got totally winded. I slung one arm over the gutter to hold myself up and wailed between breaths, "I can't figure it out! What's wrong with me?"

Besides being an athlete, Debra is also a truth-teller.

"This isn't about the swimming," she said. "Your swimming is fine. Something else inside of you is making it hard for you to breathe. You need to breathe. You know how. Now do it."

And standing in the shallow end of the pool, tears and snot running down my face, and lifeguards and other swimmers looking on, Deb prayed with me. After that, I know what makes it hard to breathe because I remember a particular day in the pool. I'm just about twelve and getting ready for gym class my first day at Woodland Junior High School. I've just moved to a new small city from a little place on an island, where I learned to swim in lakes, not in pools. In fact, I've spent a lot of my life splashing into lakes and paddling around, or hopping up and down on one foot to avoid leaches. But I never logged much pool time—certainly never enough time to swim an actual lap!

My legs are completely ridiculous in the scratchy slow-drying black swimsuit I've been issued for class. They are as white as the snow outside, for one thing, and as long as a stork's. The only way I can think to solve this problem is to hide them, and the only way to hide them is by keeping my bumpy knee socks on.

I've been assured I don't have to swim, since it's my first day, but the walk to the bleachers by myself is just as confounding as swimming a lap would have been. I didn't reckon on the floor of the pool deck being so wet. The wet soaks the soles of my socks and then slowly, ever so slowly, wicks up, dampening my wet socks halfway up to my knobby knees. It feels like I'm tortuously wetting my pants in reverse, and I'm sure everyone else can tell, too.

The fear that had made me breath-less is not not-being-able-to-swim fear, but everyone-will-laugh fear.

I guess there are other, more primal fears, but if I scratch the surface of many of my fears, everyone-will-laugh is at the root. When I was in classes at Woodland Junior High, I learned that there are two reactions to fear—fight or flight. Jaimal Yogis, author of the book *The Fear Project*, says that scientists now identify three—fight, flight, or freeze. "Fear won't go away. Fear is there for a reason, a survival tool. But we can change how we react and view our most primal emotion. It can be a huge deal that becomes literally what we are. Or it can just be an occasional flicker on the ocean of mind."[2]

Over the years, fear was more than a flicker; it was what I was, how I defined myself. Now, I'm still afraid sometimes, but not every minute like I was for so many years. Fear didn't win this one. After my lesson

---

2. I love his book (Emmaus, PA: Rodale Books, 2013). But if you can't commit to a whole book, this actual quote comes from Jaimal Yogi's much shorter article at Huffington Post: http://www.huffingtonpost.com/jaimal-yogis/fear-project_b_1512298.html.

with Deb, I got in the pool and actually swam, except when I rolled back and looked up, thinking about being a mermaid. Which is pleasant, but this is no time for dreaming. We are touring, so let's continue the tour. It is time to heave out of the pool, shower again, pull clothes on over damp, sticky skin and head out to another part of the gymnasium—the room where they keep the stationary bikes.

Can you find me? I'm the one with the grin on her face, pumping her legs with all her might. When it's going well—and this is my tour, so let's imagine that it is going well—I can keep up a steady rate of eighty-five rotations per minute for thirty minutes, which is medium slow for a real cyclist, but amazing for me. More than once a second, much more quickly than it takes to read these words, my thighs pull up and my calves push up and then they both swing around and down and my legs have formed another circle, and another, and another.

My husband, Jeff, has a machine we call the bicycle, too. Let's add Jeff's bike to this room of the imaginary gymnasium so you can see it. It's not a bicycle like mine. In order for Jeff to use his bike, I kneel down and strap his feet to the pedals, and a motor moves his legs in a circle and then another and another. Jeff has what is broadly called muscular dystrophy. His more specific diagnosis is called by its proper name, spinal muscular atrophy, or its nickname, SMA.

Jeff was already in a wheelchair a decade and half ago when we crossed the lines of friendship to become lovers, but at the time I hardly noticed. What I did notice was his indomitable intellect, patience, beautiful eyes, depth, candor, artistic talent, remarkably deep speaking voice, air of complete trustworthiness, spiritual curiosity, unexpectedly vigorous laugh, the surprising sweetness of the tiny sound he made when sneezing.

And the kissing.

I'd done quite a lot of kissing before but I'm pretty sure I didn't really get the point of it until I bent near Jeff to pick something up and he put his hand on the back of my head and kissed me for the first time.

I know what you see when you look at the pair of us. You see a woman who never stops moving, whose legs go around and around and around. And you see a man strapped to a machine. Stay here with us in this room for a while. Things are both more and less complicated than you imagine. On our ride, sometimes we coast, sometimes we pedal, sometimes we push uphill. I will show you. But, for now, let's move on. We have another room to visit on the tour of the gymnasium.

Unlike the transition from pool to bicycle, I don't have to change clothes when I move to the track. But I might change, thinking it will help. I might do other things. I might lace my shoes tighter. Lace them looser. Get advice. Warm up before. Warm up after. Take two pills. Put on a warm-up jacket. Take it off. Get some different advice. Try a new bra. Wear an inspiring t-shirt. Put smart podcasts on the headphones, or music or prayers.

It won't matter what I do; it will hurt.

I thought I just didn't feel like it, that's why I didn't run. I didn't know it would hurt. A lot of people I know run, and it doesn't seem to hurt them. I can picture myself at eight, standing in front of the kitchen cupboard, the bottom one designed to hold the big pots. It doesn't hold pots. Instead, it's crammed with cases of granola bars. Should I have cinnamon? Or honey oat? I can choose either, or both; there will be plenty more —enough to last for months, enough so I will actually get sick of them. What are people both as health-conscious and as poor as my parents doing with cases of sugary snacks? That's because, for a while, my dad both ran (as in organized) and ran (as in ran) a marathon on our little island. And the granola bars are the leftovers. There have always been runners in my life. Runners, running.

My grandfather had the hearty name Maranatha Sleight Garrison. His name sounds a little like "marathon" but really means "come, Lord Jesus!" Scholars wonder if this untranslatable word is a prayer or a curse. Maybe it's both. Maranatha seemed old and frail by the time I knew him, decimated by diabetes, strokes, heart attacks, and perhaps some unspoken disappointment. In his younger days, my great-uncle remembers that Maranatha was a runner, remembers his long legs stretching down the dusty roads of India, where his missionary parents raised him. My dad does not remember his father running, but, along with pastoring, running was encoded in my dad's DNA.

Since I can remember, my dad's been a runner and a pastor too. Sometimes dad was a runner who did not run, but instead smoked cigarettes and lifted firewood and hassled my brothers into shoveling the walk with him. But in those days, I still thought of him as a runner. I just thought of him as a runner who did not run. I guess those things must be encoded in my DNA, too. The pastor part I picked up, the running part didn't take somehow.

One year, my dad and a family friend ran a marathon the day before we went camping together. Our friend did not come out of her tent much during the camping trip because, her husband explained, her toenails had turned black and were falling off one by one. I thought this was gross, but I did not think about how it would, you know, hurt.

Walking? I can walk for miles, for hours. Every time I train I think that I'm not sure why running is so different, why it hurts like it does. I think of Maranatha Sleight, his long legs churning the dust. I think of my dad, kicking his smoking habit for the third, fourth, fifth time with tiny pieces of Trident gum broken into even tinier quarters and chewed one at a time. I think of him returning from a run, propping his shoes against the back door, stretching out. I imagine I am doing it wrong, but I cannot seem to do it right. Every now and then, I get a little rush, the endorphin high that other runners talk about. But mostly, running is just something to be endured. Here in my imaginary gymnasium, I grit my teeth and do a lap, or two, or three.

After that, we limp toward the little quiet corner where rolled-up mats lean against the wall in neat stacks. I take one down and sit on it. Breathe in, breathe out. This is the special place and time for quieting, as the yogis say, the mind-body. Breathing. In and out. In and out.

It has not always been this easy. More times than I can count when Elijah was small, I called the nurse hotline to report, "My baby is having a hard time breathing." The first thing the faceless nurse on the other end of the line always asks: "Is he blue?"

What I think is, "If the baby were *blue*, do you think I would dig around in my wallet to find the white insurance card hidden behind all the other white cards, call an 800 number, and follow a labyrinth of voice prompts to get to a human at last? Would I do all that to get to you, and ask you what to do if the child were *blue*? Wouldn't I instead wrap the baby in the stars quilt the church ladies made for him? Wouldn't I run into the street holding him above my head and keening? If the baby were blue, a more primal response than a call to the nurse hotline seems to be in order."

That is what I think. But what I say is, "No, the baby is not blue." Then I describe the symptoms to her as calmly as I can and listen while the nurse on the other end tells me that, yes, it is time to go to the hospital. Now. Again.

The baby is not blue today. The baby is a very sturdy ten-year-old. Those times are past. Breathe. In and out. In and out.

Athletic endeavor is not merely like life. Athletic endeavor is life. This is a cliché, I have discovered much to my surprise halfway through my life, that is actually true.

I thrash and gasp and eventually move forward. As in the pool, so in my life.

Other times, my legs go around and around and I fly forward without, it seems, any effort. As on the bicycle, so in my life.

Sometimes, things just hurt and no amount of preparation or advice can make them better. Only time and rest can do that. As in running, so in my life.

My body knows how to breathe, the lungs rising and falling, in and out. Sometimes I forget. I hold my breath. I choke. As in tri training, so in life.

The tri was not, as I thought for a few months after the training, the end of things. My knee would heal, and I would continue to stretch and swim and move. As I took one step forward, one step back in my body, my spirit did, too. As a pastor, my work absorbs many hours of my waking days and often occupies my dreams, too. I thought I was getting into tri training to put all that church stuff aside for an hour or two a day. But it didn't really work that way. The last thing I expected was that running a triathlon would help me understand my faith better, but that's just what happened.

You already know that my grandparents and their parents before them were missionaries. My dad says, when someone asks him why he sticks with it, that Christianity is his mother tongue. There are many reasons to be suspicious of Christianity, I suppose. Over the years, I've heard most of them and thought the rest. But there's at least one reason to appreciate it. Jesus came to us incarnate—in a body. My husband jokes that "incarnate" is the fancy church word for "we are all meat in a sack." But we are also so very much more than meat in a sack.

As I trained, my body got stronger, and so did my spirit. I understood some of those faith stories that previously seemed like a total mystery to me, and I tried to preach about them, explaining them to myself by explaining them to other people. So some of those Bible characters snuck unexpectedly into this writing too, a reminder that it was not just my body that got stretched, molded, transformed by training for the tri. It was my spirit, too.

The door to the gymnasium is open. Whether you have been here all your life, or last ran screaming from here in middle school and swore never to look back, welcome. Let me show you around.

part one

SWIM

I | *In Which I Jump into the Pool*

A triathlon starts in the water. Sometimes it's open water—a lake, a river, or an ocean. This triathlon, the 2012 McMinnville, Oregon Parks and Rec Department Sprint Triathlon, starts in a pool. Or maybe it starts before the pool, in the car, with Justin Bieber on the headphones and the green dawn of May in western Oregon zipping past. Or maybe it begins the night before with lists of things not to forget to pack (towel, Luna bar, helmet . . .) and then packing the things from the list and then unpacking to make sure I have everything and then repacking it again. Or maybe it begins all those months before when Dennis at church said to me, almost in passing, "It's one of the most important things in life to set a goal and then to complete it."

I thought about that and wondered if, officially in my mid-forties, it was too late to actually set a goal for the first time.

"OK," you may be thinking, "obviously, you've set and met other goals at some point in the last four decades."

It's true if you look at my life on the outside. I don't look like much of a drifter. I attended college. Twice. I got married, became a pastor, had a kid, moved to the suburbs. But the truth was, I felt always like I moved without much thought into the next thing that showed up. I felt lucky that somehow things just seemed to work out, mostly, but I did not expect that luck to last.

During that year in college when I drank too much more than a few times just to see what it was like, some boys found me late one night leaning woozily against the wall of some bar.

"Come on, honey," they cajoled, "we'll walk you home."

I thought I recognized one of the guys from a class and the idea seemed as good as any other. I squinted up at the boys, reached out a hand toward the voice and felt someone pull me, wobbly, to my feet. It seemed very hard to see any of their faces clearly, so I looked at their shirts instead, trying to make the wide stripes of white and green come into focus. At that moment, my boyfriend's roommate came out of the bar.

"She's with me. I'll walk her home." His earnest Cameroonian accent sounded more beautiful than ever. He firmly took my hand and walked faster than I could really keep up into the cool night, the stars spinning close overhead.

Later I found out that the boys in the green and white shirts were members of a rugby team who had been accused of raping another student. I thanked my escort by throwing up on his shoes on the way home and crying that he was my one true friend.

I didn't drink much after that, but you don't need alcohol to become an addict. I got addicted to drifting. I waited around for someone to come along to suggest a course of action. As long as I didn't get a better offer, I just went along with whatever was suggested.

But no one would have suggested a triathlon to me, for me. Because no one, starting most especially with myself, would have seen me as the kind of person who would do a thing like that.

Until today. I have set a goal, my own goal. I have trained for this day and prepared. I have not slept all night to make sure I would be awake when the alarm goes off at five. And now, here I am, not just at, but *in* a sprint triathlon.

I'm in the second pool at the second rec center, which is really, let's face it, the baby pool. I'm sitting on the edge next to two other people who have similar estimated swim times as I do. I assume we are the slow lane, although a few lanes over are two little girls, maybe ten or eleven years old. Surely they must be slower than us, I think with relief.

I'm surprised by how friendly and chatty my lane-mates—an incredibly tall guy a little older than me, and a woman my age named Jennifer, naturally—are. (For those of you who are not one of the million and half or so Jennifers born in the late 1960s and early 1970s, suffice to say there are a lot of us. A lot.) The tall guy tells me his name, too.

It's not Jennifer, and I instantly forget it. We agree that the first triathlon sure is nerve wracking, decide I will go first, and then run out of things of say.

We sit around.

We grin sheepishly at each other and fidget.

It seems like the race will never start and I wonder why I arrived early.

"See, this is why it's a good idea to be late for things, because then you don't have to wait for stuff to start," the most unhelpful voice in my head comments.

This part probably lasts for a minute and a half, but it feels like a lot longer. At last, a guy with a clipboard and a whistle comes by. Nothing in life has prepared me for helpful kindness from any individual carrying either a clipboard or a whistle and certainly not both, so I do what I do when I am nervous. I start talking.

"This pool, it's so small! I've been swimming in a much bigger one and I have to keep track of my laps. How will I know when I'm done? I really have to keep track of my laps in order to . . ." I go on like this for a minute or two.

My nervousness about Clipboard Dude was needless, it turns out. He waits for me to run out of steam and then taps the clipboard with confidence but with none of the aggression I expect.

"Don't worry, I mark down all the laps right here. I'll be counting all your laps and keeping track. Now, if you're going first, you should start in the water. I'll blow the whistle for you to go and then fifteen seconds later, I'll blow the whistle again and the next person will go, OK?" His smile is reassuring.

My husband, Jeff, and (as of today! It's his birthday!) ten-year-old son, Elijah, wave from the end of the lane.

I probably wave back, but I'm distracted by my brightly colored earplugs as I slide into the water. I fiddle with them, put them in my ears, worry I won't be able to hear the signal when it comes and take them out again. I'm more than a little hard of hearing. Whistles, especially high ones, are often out of my hearing range.

Then suddenly! The whistle! I did hear it after all. I've got an earplug in my right ear, the left one in my hand. I bounce with one leg on the bottom and flail with my right arm, trying to use my left hand to get the other earplug in before my head hits water.

The other whistle is blowing. Could that really have been fifteen seconds already? Other Jennifer is coming up behind me. In all the business with the earplugs, I seem to have forgotten all about my goggles, which are resting on my forehead. I continue the new stroke I have just invented, the One-Armed Thrash, while trying to get the goggles down over my eyes.

I don't know if it is the ridiculousness of the goggles, the earplugs, and the thrashing that I call swimming; the fact that I'm finally doing this thing I've been preparing for over such a long time period; or Jeff's voice calling, "Go! Go!" but I am so happy, I'm having a hard time not laughing out loud. I stop myself, though. What I definitely don't need right now is a lung full of water.

By the end of the short length, I am already out of breath, but I have left off the One-Armed Thrash and am swimming for real. Other Jennifer and Tall Guy are close behind. I grab the wall, push off and swim the length back to the guy with the clipboard. I count one. I hope Clipboard Dude does, too.

One down, some number I don't know to go. In the big pool, it would be ten total laps for five hundred meters; in this smaller pool I'm not sure. Clipboard Dude had told us that it was a certain number of laps and then one length, to make five hundred meters, but in the way of numbers, the exact amount is already out of my head. I guess I just need to keep going until he says to stop.

I swim another length. Other Jennifer and Tall Guy are just behind me. I've been learning about swimmer's etiquette, so I nod, say, "Go ahead," just as if we were at a leisurely lap-swim practice at my pool at home instead of an actual race.

Wow, Tall Guy sure has an advantage when it comes to pushing off the side of the pool. One push takes him almost halfway across. Wait a minute; he's rolling on his back! I didn't know before that it was permitted in an actual race situation to use the backstroke, but I do now and I'm delighted. The backstroke is totally my speed.

With a combination of the splash-and-kick I call swimming, and the backstroke, I keep going back and forth until at last I hear the Clipboard Dude tell me that when I finish the next length, I am done.

I swim back across the short pool, clamber out, and look around. I am the very last person out of the pool, including the little girls, but I'm so stoked I actually don't care. I'm one-third done and next is my favorite part—biking. I'm the last one out of the pool, and all I can think is, "I'm doing this! I can't believe I'm really doing this!"

As I trot out of the pool, I high-five some women waiting for their wave to start.

In the pictures I look at later, I'm grinning. In the ones from before the start, my smile is stretched and nervous. But the minute the race started, teeth is all you can see in the pictures. My grin looks relaxed, confident, and proud. The rest of me is a blur, moving through the water.

2 | *A Whole Lotta Deep*

I remember another pool, another grin. But it's me, grinning up at my brother Noah. He crouches on the edge of the pool and looks down, as if for the first time. Unexpectedly, he pauses in our game of "jump-and-I'll-catch-you" and shudders in the warm sun. Noah's lifejacket, which he wears because he can't swim yet, is dripping water from many jumps before.

In water, I love that I can catch him mid-flight and pull him close to me, a feat my stick-thin arms can never accomplish on land. I love the standing-on-tiptoe-floaty feeling, combined with the reassuring solidness of the concrete pool floor, and the fluid, secure embrace of the water. I love the hot sun on my head. I love the laughter and splash that comes with each jump.

Mostly, though, I love being counted on. Love being the catcher of jumpers.

"Is this your son?" someone had asked me when they saw me with Noah, and I loved that at thirteen to my brother's three, I looked mature enough to be a mother.

"She's so *good* with the little ones," I overhear the grownups say to each other, and I love most of all to be *good*, and to have the *good* noticed.

Noah was still the baby because Jacob hadn't been born yet. So it was he and I and our brother Mark who were in Florida with our parents, visiting Grammy, the retired teacher and missionary. Grammy—who whacked diabetic Maranatha with a fly swatter if he went near a piece of pie, but handed us oatmeal cookies for breakfast; who organized packs of grandkids into an ad hoc choir when we gathered each summer; who potty-trained me on another visit a decade before, my mom recalls some-what mysteriously, "with a pack of gum." Grammy, who is sick now, her head surprisingly bald under the red wig she chose because, "I always wanted to be a redhead, and now I am!"

But I'm not thinking of Grammy now. Noah is all I can see and I'm squinting up at him into the sun.

"JumpandI'llcatchyou!" I cry.

"Are you *sure* this is the shallow end?" Noah's three-year-old voice quavers.

"Yes, I'm sure. Come on! Jump! I'll catch you!" And I will, too. Even at thirteen, I am nice like that, and responsible.

Noah shivers again. He says, "There's a whole lotta deep down there."

I know why he shivered when he looked into deep water. Being in the water, half floating on my tippy toes, I didn't feel it. But I knew what it was like to stand on the edge, to see the whole lotta deep down there. In those moments, I got that same thrill, that same shiver of awe.

And, although I was ten years older than him, and secure on my tippy toes on the solid bottom of the pool, the truth was I couldn't swim either. Not for years and years, not until I was an adult and I started training for the tri.

THE BREATH JOURNALS: PART I

Once at a hotel pool, I saw a woman speaking with subdued viciousness to her children while they prepared to swim and then tried to follow her many directions to not run, not splash, be nice to your sister. But when asked, she bent tenderly over the stick-thin arms of her little son and blew into the valve of his water wings, so he could float.

Ever since, I've wished I were a poet, so I could write a poem about it. About how the mother bent her head over the son, how the movement of her breath reminded me of the suckling that had sustained him once. If I were a poet, I would know if that was a good metaphor or not.

I would know how to write about how, even on the days when our resentment is deepest, we feed our children with our bodies, and then later hold them up with our own strong, ephemeral breath, and then, last of all, send them out into the water to feed and breathe on their own.

3 | *Lake Superior Did Not Teach Me to Swim*

I want to tell the truth and already I've told half of one. It isn't strictly true that I could not swim at all.

I spent the intense late childhood years we now call tween on Madeline Island in Lake Superior, the largest of the northern chain called the Great Lakes, the third largest body of fresh water in the whole world. Crouched on the tiny rocks that made up the beach, hugging my knees, looking out over the horizon, I would ache to swim out as far as I could, until I was myself water, or at least a water creature. A mermaid perhaps, if mermaids could have survived in a lake whose surface freezes solid in winter, warms only slightly in the summer.

When I say I couldn't swim, I meant I didn't swim laps in a pool. That didn't stop me from spending as much time as possible splashing in the shallows during those short, northern Wisconsin summer months.

My brothers and I loved that breathtaking water, running across the street from the church parsonage to the beach as often as we were allowed. Noah's first sentence, "Trow rocks in da water," was his constant request.

The lake was our big playmate, but a dangerous one. Three or four boys I knew, shoveling a circle onto the ice one winter day, looked back to shore to realize that the ice floe they had chosen for their hockey rink had drifted from shore. Later when I asked them about it at school, they didn't want to talk about it. The adults said the boys jumped into the water, weighed down by heavy black boots and snowmobile suits. They made it to shore, but the story as my classmates and I heard it over and over that winter, always ended with, and was punctuated by frequent *and-they-could have-died*s.

"There's a whole lotta deep down there."

I did not like being scared. Even in high school I spent some slumber party or other lying behind the couch pretending to nonchalantly page through a magazine while my friends watched a horror movie. I wonder, though, if it was because of the thrill, the fear, that I loved Lake Superior so much. Loved with a thrill of horror the mystery of the lamprey eel that haunted the waters, leaving quarter-sized holes in the sides of fish. Loved the pebbly beach, hard under our toes. Loved even the shifting, treacherous ice and the secret knowledge only we island people had of the safest way to drive across it in winter.

The Lake would freeze enough to drive on sometime after the first of the year, after the island's two hundred or so winter residents piled our discarded Christmas trees out on the ferry dock. Then Someone used those trees to mark the safest route a couple of miles from Madeline Island to Bayfield, two and half miles across the water.

Every year, there was Someone Else who didn't wait long enough or who thought he knew a faster way than the one marked out by . . . Whom? I'm not sure who would have taken this terrible responsibility. The competencies of adults were as mysterious as the Lake herself. For example, there were those adults careful and clever enough to know exactly how to mark out a safe path over ice. And then there were those impatient or drunken adults who would speed or wander off the marked way and get hung up on the soft, black slush.

"It doesn't happen all at once, losing your car in in the Lake," Hester (not her real name) said. "First you get stuck in the slush." She was telling my brother Mark and me about a car she actually saw go down this way. Hester was in auto parts, so she knew a lot about cars.

"As soon as he was stuck, he rocked it, forward, back, forward, back. But he panicked, gunned it, and then that car was a goner. Nothing to do now but get out, stand back, watch it go under."

Then hapless Whoever-It-Was turned up his collar and hoofed toward shore before he froze to death.

She told us this, and many other stories, in the years we knew and loved her. Hester, the very first person who visited the parsonage the very first day we got to Madeline Island, was our initiator into island life. We'd moved there so my dad could take a job as a pastor of the little Protestant church. We were still surrounded by unpacked boxes when she knocked at the door.

"Mom, was that a *man*?" we asked as soon as the door was closed behind Hester's cropped hair and all-denim outfit. That day, she gave my mom a check for $100 and us kids a lesson, too. Besides early instruction in gender identity, we also learned that we were poor, but not everyone was. Later, Hester and her friend-who-lives-with-her Norma (not her real name, either) also taught us how to find a golf ball in the rough, play backgammon, groom an Afghan hound, cook a steak (with a pat of butter), love the music of Waylon Jennings. Hester taught my nine-year-old brother Mark how to drive a boat on the water in summer and how to drive a car on the ice in winter.

Of course, we couldn't drive on the ice all the time. In the summer, we rode ferries. I guess we must have ridden for free because, in my memory, I go back and forth all day, feeling the wind in my hair and the thrum of the engine, watching the wake trail out behind me, making up stories in my head about when I would be grown up and married to a ferry captain, someone steady, silent, strong, sexy.

In between the season of water and the season of ice was the season of slush. Then the Lake was an undercooked cake not ready to come out of the oven. In these times, the ice was too thick for the ferries to plow through—but not ready to drive on. Then we took the iceboat. The iceboat was really an open fishing boat with an airplane engine jammed on the back, which gave it enough lift so it bumped and skittered across the ice.

Every time we bundled into the iceboat, my mom winced from the noise and cold, held baby Noah's hooded head to protect his little ears, his eyes across the boat from me wide with shock. My mom, I realize now as I did not then, hated the iceboat. She hated it even though she was not there the time my dad stepped out of the iceboat onto the slushy side instead of the solid ice side. She hated it even though she did not see dad clamber out of ice water up to his thighs, holding baby Noah over his head and soaking his khaki pants.

Lake Superior was dangerous all right. But that did not stop me from loving "the Lake" as we always called her, the way New Yorkers call New York "the City," as if now that you've seen this one, you won't ever need another. The Lake was mine, and I was hers. But she wasn't friendly, wasn't a place for swimmers. And although I spent hours, days, whole summers paddling on her edges, I didn't swim much. So when did it start, then? This urge to swim?

I liked being in water—floating, paddling, goofing around. But I didn't ever think I could swim, I mean *really swim*, until years later, when I was a full-grown adult. It happened one Christmas Day, by accident. It was small-ish as accidents go. My big dog knocked me over while she romped with another dog at the park. I limped home to lie on the couch moaning for a day or two until my husband suggested a visit to a doctor might be in order.

The doc looked at my swollen knee, told me it wasn't that bad and suggested either physical therapy or deep-water aerobics. This was a year or two before I had heard of or imagined that one day I would do a triathlon, but I knew for sure I didn't want to go to PT because Jeff had one time had a toe broken at a physical therapy appointment. I was not a swimmer, but I chose the water. Deep-water aerobics it was.

4 | *What Is Impossible?*

That first day of deep-water aerobics class, and for many days afterward, I strapped a wide blue foam belt around my waist, grabbed some foam barbells to further hold me above water, and crept cautiously into the neighborhood pool.

A few times, I was uncharacteristically early to class and saw the lap swimmers finishing up. They were sea otters to my tree sloth. They were graceful, gorgeous, slender. I was large, clumsy, already planning my next snack. I could never be them, I thought, never. And, at first, I didn't really want to be like them, because water aerobics was a revelation. It was exercise I could do, and not only *do*, but actually enjoy more than a little.

This particular class had no regular teacher. The lifeguards—college students paying off bills and eager for a break from the relative boredom of lifeguarding—rotated leading us through the exercises.

One of the lifeguards sort of scared me. When he jumped into the pool and then bobbed back up, the water streamed off his buzz cut like the ocean off a seal's back. His tattoos of tiki huts and palm trees were magnified by drops of chlorinated water. And, unlike the rest of the lifeguards who doubled as instructors, he was very serious about water aerobics.

It's not easy to be serious about water aerobics. For one thing, the uniform of water aerobics lacks any of the badass qualities of other sports. A sturdy swimsuit. That wide foam belt for buoyancy. Maybe a pair of those flimsy water shoes. Perhaps a swim cap with flowers on it, with a strap that snaps under the neck (yes, they do still make those).

For another thing, the class was made up, not of athletes, but of people like me who had been offered aerobics as an alternative to physical therapy for some injury or another. People like me, sure, only with four or five decades more life experience. One day, waiting for the shower, I overheard one water aerobist confess to another, "I don't know how to tell my daughter this, but I'm ninety years old and I don't think a new washing machine is really what I need."

This particular lifeguard, though, did not seem to notice that we were old, feeble, only here to avoid some more painful treatment for our various ailments. You could tell he thought of water aerobics as a real sport. He was our coach and we were not just trying to push back time, stretch out knees, back, and hips. To him, we were serious athletes. He harangued us if he caught us trying to sneak out of the pool early to hit the showers before they got too crowded.

"If you miss the cool-down, the whole effect of your workout is ruined," he scolded.

Maybe it was because he was so serious himself and took us so seriously that the class all liked him. We liked that, unlike some of the instructors who yelled directions at us from a perch on the diving board, he got right in the water with us like we were all athletes together. We took turns tsk-tsking over his newest tattoo, asking about his girlfriends, trying to get him to laugh.

I wasn't in that aerobics class long before I heard that our favorite lifeguard was leaving, moving to Hawaii. Water aerobics leaves plenty of time and breath for gossip.

One of the ladies who, to my wonder, came to class in full make-up and coiffed hair, nodded to me as I bobbed past.

"He's going to teach surfing," she confided.

"I think there's a girl there," her equally coiffed friend loudly whispered.

After class a few weeks later, we changed into dry clothes and held a little farewell potluck for him in the cheerless party room in the basement of the rec center.

"Surfing, huh?" I made small talk over plates of cut melon and crockpot meatballs.

"Yes," he replied as he offered one of his rare smiles.

"You know," I said, in the way of extroverts trying a thought out loud before it is fully formed, "I don't do other sports like downhill skiing, but I look at them and I can imagine doing them, you know? I can understand them, I mean. I think, 'If I practiced and got strong I could do that.' But I look at surfing and I can't even imagine what it takes. I think surfing is magic."

Another smile! "It feels like magic, too."

"Do you think you could teach *me* to surf?" I blurted out, typically, before I knew what I was saying.

He was thoughtful again for an instant. "Yes, I could."

"Except. I can't get my head wet."

"Well. That would make it harder."

"And. I don't know how to swim."

"Well, no, then. You can't learn to surf."

Then he was gone. To Hawaii—a place that seemed as mythical to me as surfing itself. But the idea stayed, the question did not go away. Could I really learn how to surf? I would have to start with what probably seemed to the lifeguard like small steps, but which to me seemed like insurmountable obstacles.

I would have to put my head under water.

I would have to learn how to swim.

5 | *The Problem Is the Ears*

I mean, I knew how to keep afloat, to dog paddle around. But before I started training for the triathlon, I cannot remember ever actually swimming a whole lap in a pool.

It's not fear of the water. It's my ears, see. I'm that kid the doctors had to hold down, screaming, as they put ear tubes in and took them out, put them in again and then took out a second time. (My son has spent a lot of time in and out of hospitals, but luckily never has been plagued with earache, so I don't know if they still do this as they did in the medieval days when I was a child.)

I'm the kid who spent that one precious day at Disneyland in the infirmary, laid up with an ear infection. Should have been more careful playing jump-and-I'll-catch-you, the doctors guessed. I stopped putting my ears in the water after that.

Even out of water, my ears continued to be a problem. For several years in my mid-thirties, daily headaches went undiagnosed until a physical therapist stopped them by showing me the Epley maneuver, a short series of movements of head and body designed to jar something she described as "little stones" back into the ear canal.

"Your body hates being dizzy so much that it would rather give you a headache than feel dizzy," she said.

No doctor had been able to say why my hearing started failing at age thirty, but those early ear problems probably had something to do with it. Commiserating about wearing hearing aids is a good icebreaker, I have found, with the older folks in my church. Hearing aids help me understand the conversations that, without them, sound like so much mumbling. But they don't do anything to stop the "little stones" from rolling out of place, don't stop my ears from aching in even the mildest wind.

How could I get my head under water without getting them wet? I tried one over-the-counter earplug after another. But they were uncomfortable and they leaked a little. I mentioned this to the hearing aid technician on a check-up and his face broke into a smile.

"I can help you with that! I can make some plugs that will mold right into your ears."

Elijah happened to be with me on that visit. He was cruising the office, putting his hand out toward the sparkling equipment, looking at me and then stopping when I shook my head at him.

"What color do you want?" The technician asked. To give him something to do, I let Elijah choose. He chose purple and pink swirled together and then we hurried out of the office on another errand. I didn't think too much about the earplugs until they came in the mail a few weeks later.

"Sure aren't gonna lose those things in the water," Jeff deadpanned when I shook them out of their little container. And it's true; they were very bright, clashed ridiculously with my yellow and green suit. But I didn't care. With them in, I hoped I could put my head under the water.

I took Elijah to the neighborhood pools on the weekend and practiced, holding my breath until my cheeks puffed all the way out and then bobbing up and down. At first, I covered the earplugs with both hands to make sure they would stay in, but over time I grew more confident. I let go with both hands and the earplugs did not fall out, did not allow a waterfall to rush into my ears.

It was time to learn how to swim a lap.

THE BREATH JOURNALS: PART II

When someone gets a song in his or her head and says, "I have an earworm," I wince a little, shake my head, think of the tiny stones. I wish I knew another word for that, but don't. My earworm these days is thanks to Peter Mayer. Sometimes Jeff and I tease each other, hum a few bars of some eighties techno song, trying to plant an earworm. Unlike the silly songs we try to trick each other into getting stuck with, this one actually feels good to carry around, a little living thing that hums somewhere deep in my throat.

When holy water was rare at best
It barely wet my fingertips.
Now I have to hold my breath
Like I'm swimming in a sea of it.[3]

---

3. Peter Mayer, "Holy Now," © 1999 Peter Mayer.

6 | *Why My Husband Can't Swim*

I've given it a lot of thought, but I'm not entirely sure what pushed me to take those first ambitious strokes across the pool. I know part of it, though. Part of it was Jeff.

When he was a kid, Jeff loved to swim, but he no longer has the strength or endurance for it. Swimming is just more one item on the long List of Things Jeff Cannot Do. Other items on the list: pull on his socks, pick up a full plate of food, accept an invitation to the neighbor's three-stepped house. These items had been written in stone, carved there by a condition that robs him of his energy and saps his strength more and more day by day. My List of Things Jennifer Cannot Do was pretty long, too. If I were honest with myself, many of the items on that list were there because I put them there. Jeff's muscular dystrophy made it impossible for him to do many things. My own thoughts made it impossible for me to do many more. He wanted to swim and physically could not. I wanted to swim but was scared to try.

Seattle University's School of Theology and Ministry, the seminary where I studied to be a pastor, allowed spouses of students to audit one class per quarter for free. The second quarter we looked over the listings together and Jeff decided to join me in World Religions with a visiting professor. The first night, we found a place to sit on the edge of the room, and the professor handed out the syllabus and introduced himself. He began to talk us through the course outline, his East Indian accent precise and measured. He did not get far.

"... And then for the mid-term exam ..."

Cue uproar.

"Is that a *test?*"

"We don't take tests here."

"Can I write a paper instead?"

"I have a learning disability. I can't take a test!"

It is true that the seminary did not generally include testing as part of the curriculum. We were more accustomed to papers written outside of class without the pressure of memorizing facts or watching a clock. Still, the concept of tests was not unknown, and this was, after all, graduate school. All the students in that class must have graduated from some kind of four-year university. Very real learning disability not withstanding, it is not presumptuous to assume that some tests must have been taken in those student's lives.

By the time we climbed into the van for home, Jeff was fuming that the class time had been taken up not with studies of the religions he was so curious about, but instead with an argument with a baffled visiting professor about how he should conduct the class.

"Learning disability and can't take tests!" he scoffed. "Maybe grad school isn't the right place for a person with a disability that severe. I mean, I'll never be an Olympic swimmer, either. But I recognize that. I just don't have it in me. "

He slid off the three-wheel scooter he used to get around in those days and into the van's driver's seat. With his right hand he shifted the van into reverse, while with his left hand he activated the accelerator.

I didn't realize how long my List of Things Jennifer Cannot Do really was. Before I knew Jeff, I honestly think I had never heard anyone say the words, "I just don't have it in me." The soundtrack of my childhood was "Free to Be You and Me," with Marlo Thomas's plucky assertion anyone could be anything anyone wanted to be. I worshipped freely, if carelessly, at the altar of the Church of Marlo, believing with the confidence of a middle-class white kid in in late-twentieth-century America that I could be and do pretty much anything. I had little concern for all that I did not do—shooting a basket, doing calculus, or cooking the perfect soufflé. Whatever I wanted to do, I probably could. If I wanted to. I just didn't want to, that's all.

Living with Jeff changed that. I no longer believed as thoughtlessly in ease, in accomplishment, in the certainty of success. By marrying, becoming a dad, having a career, living across the country from his family, Jeff had achieved a lot more than might have reasonably been expected of him as a child. But he rejects the image of the inspired, inspiring, disabled person who overcomes every obstacle thrown in his path. Jeff is very aware of his limits, very aware that there are certain activities that, as he says, just aren't in him.

As a kid with a form of muscular dystrophy called spinal muscular atrophy (SMA), Jeff grew up under the glare of medical lights at Mayo Clinic in his family's hometown of Rochester, Minnesota.

"Yeah, it was just like some episode of *X-Files*," he remembers. "One of those big round lights on in some dark room. And there I would be, sitting in my underwear on one of those metal tables. Doctors would bring their classes by to look at me."

Jeff was precious to the doctors and students because he was diagnosed unusually early. His family had been watching for signs that he might have MD since his older brother had it too, and survived. A couple of baby cousins—also victims of MD   had not been so lucky.

The most obvious symptom of muscular dystrophy is an atrophying of the voluntary muscles over time. In the case of ALS (Lou Gehrig's disease), another form of MD, the atrophy happens very quickly. Not in Jeff's case. With SMA, the kind of muscular dystrophy that Jeff and his brother, Andy, share, the atrophy is much slower, over a lifetime, over his whole body.

Marrying Jeff helped me realize for the first time that success could not always be achieved with will or pluck or good humor or even hard work. It required accommodation, assistance, and equipment. A wheelchair, a shower bench, hand controls for the van so he could drive. These all seemed like reasonable accommodations to us. A few years later, when our son was born a month early struggling to breathe, we embraced the hidden-till-you-need-it industry that envelopes early babies—the machinery, the medicine, the medical doctors.

What if some accommodations, though, are not reasonable? Unlike what I had believed from a childhood spent singing along to Marlo's hymns of self-actualization, living with Jeff had shown me the wisdom that comes from accepting the inevitability of certain limits. If Jeff tried, year after year, to become an Olympic swimmer, he would only frustrate himself and others. And he would use up stores of precious energy that he could be using to pursue something he could enjoy and even excel at. That's why he shook his head so furiously that night at the class of non-test-takers. He had made peace with the accommodations that were not reasonable.

Of course I didn't have anything like the disability Jeff had, but I, too, had a list. On top:

Jennifer cannot swim.

If this were a real list, this item would be followed by these sub-items, proofs if you will:

Jennifer cannot put her delicate ears in the water.
Jennifer has no endurance.
Jennifer will be out of breath in a minute.
And besides, her swimsuit is all wrong.

The first day I decided to try and swim a lap, I crossed something off that list. I let go of the edge and pushed with one leg off the side of the pool. I was about to find out whether lap swimming was something I had in me after all.

7 | *Learning by Doing Works for Swimming, Prayer, and Other Things*

I grew up going to church every Sunday. Ours was a liberal and gentle faith, one that did not require much except perhaps cheerfulness and an impulse toward liberal politics. It gave back an appreciation for lovely Tiffany stained-glass windows, the pleasures and perils of community life, and singing aloud. I gave it up in college, but soon after graduation, I started going again.

"I like it," I explained to my mostly nonchurchgoing friends, "when grownups stand up in groups and sing. Church is the only place that happens, aside from a baseball game. And in church, you don't have to wait for the seventh-inning stretch."

I was a churchgoer in a long line of churchgoers. I can see them in my mind's eye, stretching out back and back, generation after generation. My father's father, the missionary Maranatha Sleight Garrison, and his wife, my dear Grammy June Walker Garrison. Maranatha's father before him, Alleluia Irenaeus Garrison, was a missionary, too. Before them, more ministers and missionaries and Methodist circuit riders as far back as people keep track. It was illustrious stock, all right, but all those generations could not help me with a secret I carried into seminary.

I did not know how to pray anymore than I knew how to swim.

I sometimes thought I should probably try it, but the idea of praying in private seemed ridiculous at best and downright daunting at worst.

At the turning of 1999, I moved from northern Minnesota to Seattle to be with a guy I liked. Later we would joke to people who asked how we ended up there, "We just kept driving until we got as far west as we could and then we stopped." At the time, it really did seem that whimsical, that much by chance. I was new in town and didn't know anybody, so I figured I'd try to find a church. I opened a phone book because, heavens, we still had them in those days, and called around.

That's when I first met a pastor I'll call Roberta. Roberta did not look like a mystic. She looked like many other late-middle-aged women pastors familiar to me—solid, shod in comfortable shoes, hair a gray cloud around her head.

She was at St. Paul's United Church of Christ in Ballard as a guest that Wednesday night, leading a small group in some kind of meditation.

One of the reasons I had moved to Seattle was because nothing else in my life was working all that well. I didn't seem to be (as I had thought for a few confusing years) a lesbian after all. My several part-time jobs weren't going anywhere much. And, although it was an all-consuming thought in those waning days of my twenties, it didn't look like I would ever have a baby. At thirty, in a new relationship that could have gone any direction or none, I wanted to be pregnant with an ache that went beyond reason or planning, that had nothing to do with making a family and everything to do with biology.

During the meditation, Roberta urged us to ask God a question. I still didn't know anything about prayer, would not have considered prayer to be one of the tools in my box, but questions? I had lots of questions. A question was easy to access.

"Will I ever have a baby? Will I? Ever?"

Then something happened that had never happened before.

I saw God. I felt God's hand reach toward me. In my prayer's eye, that hand looked just like the hand of God that gives Adam the E.T. finger in that painting by Michelangelo. And gently, without pain or pressure, I felt the hand take hold of my womb and I heard a Voice speak. And the Voice said, "Not yet."

That was all—but it was enough. The church of my childhood prepared me for many of life's experiences, but not for a mystical one. The whole evening kind of scared me, and I wrote it off as hysteria due to the move and went back to the cozy apartment I shared with my boyfriend.

I still did not try to pray on my own.

But a year later, I had started seminary in the same haphazard way I did everything in those days, a quarter later than planned because I had forgotten to apply for financial aid. We were supposed to have a spiritual director for school and Roberta's was the one name on the list that I knew. I called to ask if I could see her again.

"Tell me," she asked after we settled in her messy, comfortable office. "What is your image of God?"

This was a question I was familiar with from school. In other words, when you close your eyes and say the word, "God," what picture do you see? An angry guy with the gray beard? A nicer guy, his Son—also bearded, but kinder? A Word? A Light?

I shared then about the meditation experience I'd had with her a year before, about the E.T. finger from the sky, the squeeze, the Voice.

"But that's not usual. Usually? I guess, God looks kind of like, well, nothing, I guess."

She was quiet for a long moment and I talked into the space she made. I looked at the tippy pile of books on the edge of the desk, not at Roberta.

"I guess, um. There used to be Moon Woman," I conceded. "But I don't see her any more."

"Tell me about Moon Woman."

"Well." My face went red and I stumbled over my words. I'd never really talked about Moon Woman before. "When, when . . . I was stressed or tired, you know? I used to close my eyes and ask for help and then Moon Woman would come . . . down, you know, out of the moon. She wore a long robe that covered her whole body and face and, and she would take me in her arms and hold me. Then I would feel better."

"Where is Moon Woman now?"

Roberta was neither laughing at me nor scolding me that Moon Woman sounded more like an imaginary friend than an image of God. I felt a little braver and forged ahead.

"Well, I asked her one time if I could see her face. And she pulled back her hood and. . ."

Another of Roberta's masterful pauses.

"And?"

I thrashed ahead, but I'm sure my explanation sounded as awkward as it felt.

"Well, I saw a skeleton face. You know, a skull? And then I opened my eyes and I never wanted to see her again, so I haven't called her again. And she doesn't come unless I call."

"Why didn't you want to see her again?"

"I guess . . . because . . . she scared me. She was so, you know, ugly."

"Well, what if we talked to Moon Woman now and asked her why she came to you like that? Would that be OK?"

"Um, OK."

I closed my eyes, and asked a question.

"Why? Why are you so ugly?"

For centuries, mystics have tried and failed to put words to experiences that are beyond words. I will not presume to try to explain what happened next in the hour between the question "why?" and writing a check with shaking hands and walking out of Roberta's office. I can't say what happened during that hour, but at the end of the hour, I knew something completely new.

I knew that God is love, which is not the same thing as God is cheerful. I knew that God is love and still life will be hard sometimes, not because either God or I am doing anything wrong but because that is just the nature of life. I knew that God is love and love means telling the truth, even when the truth is scary or, you know, ugly.

People who have used LSD tell me that one of the effects of the drug can be that everything becomes perfectly clear and sharp, much more real than usual. I left Roberta's office to walk a mile or so to meet my friend Rachel for tea and looked around me like I'd never looked around before. Suddenly, everything seemed so much more real than usual.

It was one of those surprisingly perfect, perfectly surprising spring days in Seattle. The sun was warm but not too hot, a light breeze blew. I passed a cherry tree, and I wondered how I had never noticed before the way each individual blossom was distinct and unique. I thought about how the flowers would die to make room for new trees and then new blossoms would come forth. That thought seemed to me to be both original and deeply comforting.

After that day, I knew that I knew how to pray. There would still be a lot of splashing and thrashing, but now I *could* pray and did. Before Roberta, before Jan (the spiritual director I saw after Roberta retired and moved away to live with her boyfriend in his RV somewhere in the Midwest), before other wise women who came across my path in those searching, aching days of my early thirties, if you had asked me about prayer, I would have said that I didn't have it in me.

My dad told me when he was a missionary boy in India that Grammy would pray aloud to pass the time in long car rides. Later, in seminary, I would learn her kind of prayers were called "prayers of petition"—requests for help or intervention or remembrance. "She would pray for everything and everybody," my dad joked, "down to Aunt Elvira's toenails." I thought prayer looked like this: a brave and devout woman in the front seat of the car, eyes closed and hands folded, saying aloud the names of all her loved ones, laying them out on the road behind her, like beads on a string.

I did not pray like that. But even though it looked and sounded very different, my conversations with Moon Woman were prayers as surely as Grammy's prayers of petition. My life, walking aimlessly around the streets of Seattle, waiting for my new boyfriend to get home from work, was so different from Grammy's, which I knew to be a life of purpose and dedication. Grammy and I at thirty had different lives, on different sides of the globe, but we were alike, too. We both had it in us. We were, both of us, calling out, asking for help, trying to remind our souls as best as we knew how that we were part of something bigger than our little selves, both of us swimming out, as best we could, into the big ocean of Spirit.

THE BREATH JOURNALS: PART III

I have two prayers these days.

One for courage, one for comfort.

>*First, for COURAGE: I breathe.*

>*Breathe in Wildness.*
>*Breathe out Goodness.*
>*Breathe in Wildness.*
>*Breathe out Goodness.*
>*And I say,*
>*The scripture tells me*
>*I was made in your Image, Holy One.*
>*So, like you,*
>*I am also Wildness, also Goodness.*
>*Breathe in Wildness,*
>*Breathe out Goodness.*

>*For COMFORT: I say these two words.*

>*Jesus. Yes.*

Sometimes, the first is tentative, uncertain, wondering, and wandering: Jesus?

And the answer, resonant and powerful and clear:

Yessss.

Other times, the name is strong, and the answer is not the divine voice, but my own small one, calling back into a darkness that I hope is fuller of light than it seems in that minute.

JESUS!

yes?

The monks and mystics say that the Divine is within, without, all around. I pray that this is true, that my "yes," the tentative small one, and Christ's "Yessss," the big and bold one, are really one and the same.

Two prayers. One for courage, one for comfort. Although, when it comes right down to it, maybe comfort and courage are really one and the same thing.

8 | *Believing Is Believing*

So Roberta moved away, and I found a new spiritual director. I liked the way Jan prayed with me. She began prayer conversationally, with none of the deep intonation I associated with prayer.

"Well, Jesus, here we are," she would begin, as if she were talking to Someone in the chair next to her, instead of Someone on High.

"Sometimes," I whispered in our second or third meeting, "The path to God feels so narrow. I don't know if I even believe in God. And if I don't believe, I don't know how I can be a minister."

"Oh," she replied with the wave of her hand that I already knew meant that she felt I was taking myself too seriously, "You're standing with one foot on the dock and one foot in the boat. Just get in the boat."

When I got home that night, I told Jeff I felt like I had on that astounding afternoon with Roberta and Moon Woman. The world tilted, shifted, and then righted itself again, completely new.

Until now, I had had it backward. The dock of disbelief I stood on was not a sturdy structure as I had thought, but small and confining, built of the unsteady planks of fear and doubt and worry. Getting into the boat, really committing to a life of faith, was like moving out onto a fast-moving river. And I was not alone on that river. With Jan's words, I saw that there were others, too, each in his or her own vessel and paddling on in his or her own way. All more or less headed in the same direction.

It wasn't easy all the time. I still thrashed and splashed more than I would have liked, and some days all I got was a lung full of water for my efforts. But something was shifting. Praying was moving, most days at least, off of the List of Things Jennifer Cannot Do.

Our son, Elijah, was small when I was learning how to pray, and he was learning new things all the time, too. At an early age, he had a lot of questions about football, something that neither Jeff nor I knew much about. A high school boyfriend had once said to me with real serious concern, "You'll never get married if you don't learn *something* about football."

I solved that problem by marrying someone who is, if possible, less interested in football than I am. Anyway, with no football experts in the house and a three-year-old who was raring to play, I did what I usually do when I want to learn about something new and there is no expert readily at hand.

I went to the library.

Armed with a book about football, I herded the book, the ball, and the boy out into the backyard. With the book in my left hand, I squinted at the text and read aloud about how to throw a spiral while trying unsuccessfully to throw one with my right. I looked up from deep concentration at my little son's expression of kind perplexity, laughed, put down the book and the ball, and then went inside and signed him up for sports camp at the local rec center. Sometimes there's no substitute for just doing a thing. All the reading in the world won't get you there.

In the decade that followed the failed attempt with the football, I kept learning, unlearning, and relearning that studying something is no substitute for doing it. In the months before I started training for the triathlon, I spent a lot of time reading about it. *Best Diet for Women Triathletes. Four Core Core Strengtheners. How to Warm Up and Cool Down.* At first I loved reading about training for the tri. The more I read, though, the more I realized that I could not learn to swim with a book in one hand. I canceled *How To Train for Your First Triathlon* from on-hold status at the library and went to the pool.

I struggled three times a week through what I sometimes grandly called "swimming laps" but more often and more accurately called "thrashing and choking."

Many days, it seemed pointlessly hard.

"Why can't I do it right?" I asked the lifeguard, pointing to the effortless swimmer gliding in the next lane. "I mean, look at that guy. He makes it look so easy!"

"Well, he's relaxed," the lifeguard replied. "That's the key. Relax."

That spring, I took a couple of lessons from friends. One Saturday, during lap swim at the pool, I watched other swimmers under water, trying to copy their long stretched arms, their effortless kicks, their regular steady breathing.

The next morning I went to my church and told everyone a story about Jonah.

"Even if you've never read the Bible at all, you may associate the name Jonah with the guy who spent some time in the belly of a whale," I told them. "Of all the people in the Bible, it's likely that the name Jonah is familiar to you, even if nothing else is. If you read his story a time or two, it's easy to see why."

Jonah reminded me of a class on existentialism I took as a tenth grader. Fifteen years old is a very existential age, so maybe that's why so many of the lessons from that class have stuck with me. Existentialism, we learned, was the philosophical response of moderns to the technology and violence of the twentieth century. This response contained elements of despair, cynicism, and ennui—that combination of boredom and anxiety so familiar to fifteen-year-olds and French philosophers. (The class introduced me to a favorite word and one I deliberately pronounced for many years with more like six n's than two, as in *ahnnnnnnnn-we*.)

"Jonah was an existentialist all right," I told the people at church that spring Sunday. "He saw the problem, recognized the solution, but then, instead of being able to act, fell into a state of despair. And he whined. I call him whiny, but really, who could blame him? God told him to go to Nineveh, a city filled with his enemies, and tell them about God. He didn't want to. I have to honestly say I wouldn't want to do that either."

So, Jonah runs away from God and gets on a boat to sail to the ends of the earth, to somewhere, anywhere where God is not. A storm blows up. The soldiers on the boat, desperate to find someone, anyone, to blame for the storm, cast lots and the lot falls to Jonah. At last realizing there is no escaping God, Jonah tells the sailors to throw him overboard, where he is immediately swallowed by a great fish.

That's the first chapter of the book of Jonah and probably the most familiar part. The second chapter is a long poem, a song that Jonah sings in the belly of the whale.

"I can relate to other things about Jonah, but it is his song that makes me admire him. Jonah acts irresponsibly, even despicably, both before and after this moment, but for now, he sings beautifully of all the hardship that has followed him this far, and then he sings with gratitude for being saved," I said.

You know, in the belly of a whale.

Others of us might panic, might on a good day think, "Well. Here we go. Out of the frying pan and into the fire."

But Jonah realizes that God is helping him out here. His smelly, cramped, and uncomfortable quarters are God's way of doing the best that God can for the moment. Jonah's life is hardly better than it was before. In fact, in many ways it is worse. But he is able to summon up an unexpected emotion—gratitude.

"Waters were at my throat," he sings. "The deep surrounded me. . . . I sank down. . . . But you, God, brought my life up from the pit."

Jonah relaxed into God at the same time as he squirmed and whined. Lapping back and forth in the pool, I could relate to the squirming and the whining. I was trying to get a handle on the relaxing.

Besides relaxing, the difficult thing with swimming is to get the breath right, turning the head at just the right time. It's imperative to fully empty the lungs. It is not intuitive, for me at least, to fully empty my lungs. I always want to hold a little bit of oxygen in there, to save it for later.

But long exhalations really help in swimming. As best as I can understand intellectually, once your lungs are fully emptied, then they can be completely filled up again with fresh, invigorating oxygen. My brain knows this, but my body does not always believe it. Also, at first it was hard to know what to do with my head, how to turn it just enough but not too much.

"Waters were at my throat . . . but you brought me up . . ." I chanted in my mind as I kicked with my legs, splashed with my arms. Little by little, I found myself squirming less and whining less. Back and forth, back and forth. Relaxing.

9 | *I Used to Be Afraid of Public Speaking . . .*

During training, I started each length of the pool with a number, the number of the length I was on. That number grew gigantic in my head, the only thing I could think. My arms and legs struggled across the pool until my fingertips touched the wall on the other side and then I would count up one, the next number filling my head until my fingers touched the wall on the far side.

Especially at first, it was not easy. But I found to my surprise that I liked swimming. Swimming, there were no decisions to be made, no worries to chew on, nothing at all to consider. For twenty-five and then thirty and then forty minutes, I had nothing to do but move my body. The other twenty-four and half hours of the day were not at all like that.

I'm not a person for whom ease comes naturally. I seem to have to thrash my way to it.

"How'd you decide to become a pastor?" someone will ask.

I'll tell them how I never intended it. How I worked at everything I could think of first—a school library, a museum, a publishing company, my mom's rehab company, a health food store. All of these jobs were interesting, but they were all missing something. Almost on a whim, I went to a visiting day at a local seminary where people go to prepare for ministry.

"I'm just here to check this out." I confessed to the jolly admissions officer. "I'm not really ready to actually, you know, be a pastor. Maybe later, when I'm ready, I'll come back.

The admissions guy laughed uproariously.

"People are never ready to give their lives to God. You just have to do it."

I took his words to heart and decided to apply. The transition was, unsurprisingly since it was me, bumpy. Before seminary actually started, I took a kind of practice Bible class in the sunny fellowship hall of the neighborhood church. In the mail, someone sent me a Denise Levertov poem that I thought would go with the texts we were studying in the class. Arriving a few minutes early, I showed it to the teacher. He glanced at it and agreed it looked interesting and invited me to read it aloud to the group.

"Me? Oh, no! Not me. I thought you could read it."

He looked at me strangely.

"You're going to seminary, right? I'm sure you can do it."

I retreated to the bathroom, tried not to cry, splashed water on my already pink face. I thought of all years stretching before me, the hours and hours and hours of talking in front of groups that was ahead of me. It was starting right now with this poem. Back in my seat, I started out, thrashing and splashing a little at the start, but eventually pulling out into longer, smoother strokes. I read them out loud, the strange words.

Given that lambs
are infant sheep,
that sheep are afraid and foolish, and lack
the means of self-protection, having
Neither rage nor claws,
. . . what then
is this 'Lamb of God'? . . .[4]

1 0 | *. . . And Many Other Things*

If you have been exercising sporadically, by which I mean not at all, then the schedule for training for a sprint triathlon is daunting. Early in the training, I found a training plan online that was developed by a man who weighed more than three hundred pounds when he started his training. The plan called for nine workouts a week or three workouts for each of the three events.

"Three hundred pounds! That's nearly twice me! If he can do it, so can I!" I exalted to Jeff on the way to bed one night.

And it was true. The first two months were more than easy. I mean, bike for fifteen minutes? It's hard to stop after only fifteen minutes on a bicycle. You're hardly getting going. It's hardly any time at all.

But the training ramped up, and so did the time spent. Instead of biking for fifteen minutes, I was on the bike for ninety minutes. Instead of swimming laps for twenty minutes, I was going two or three times that.

---

4. Denise Levertov, from "Mass for the Day of St. Thomas Didymus": "Agnus Dei," in *Candles in Babylon* (New York: New Directions, 1982), 113.

Besides the amount of time spent exercising, the rest of the training was pretty time consuming too.

Washing clothes, for example. Exercise clothes, I was horrified to realize, have to be washed pretty much every time you wear them, even if that's only for a twenty-minute workout. There's at least one extra towel to wash each day, too.

And eating. I wasn't really trying to lose weight, and I was certainly moving a lot of calories out, which meant a lot more were coming in. Which meant a lot more time spent cooking, eating, cleaning up, and even grocery shopping.

Not to mention the time spent resting, icing sore muscles, and just lying around groaning and complaining about being tired.

By the end of the training time, little piles of dust bunnies had gathered in all the corners of the house. I would schedule lunch with friends, and then cancel because I was too tired or I had missed my morning run and had to make it up in the middle of the day. Sex became waving at Jeff in the morning and evening.

"Maybe tomorrow! Gotta go work out!"

The plan I was on called for nine workouts each week. It was a choice to spend hours each week doing those things; I found I could not make that choice with ease. It weighed on me, the time lost to the training.

Many days I just thrashed and splashed, wondering if I was accomplishing much. Exercise does not feed hungry people, make the world a more verdant place, deepen relationships, answer the fifty gazillion e-mails piling up in the inbox. I read somewhere that Annie Dillard says that "how we spend our days is, of course, how we spend our lives."

"This is how I'm spending my days," I would think as I squeezed into my swimsuit before a workout.

"This is how I'm spending my life," I would think as I squelched into the rec center's communal shower to rinse off.

Many days, I followed these inspiring thoughts with, "Well, that was a waste!"

But some days, and I kept at it for those days, I would cease thrashing and splashing for a few laps at least and realize that I had, almost without thinking, crossed "swimming" pretty effectively off the List of Things Jennifer Cannot Do. If I could take swimming off the list, who knows what else could come off?

"Just relax" is some of the easiest advice to give and the hardest to accept, whether it's spoken in someone else's voice or your own. Athletes talk a lot about mind over matter, about how it's mostly mental, about how you have to think it before you can achieve it. I thought about Jeff, about his great mental capacity. I sometimes introduce him as the smartest person I know—and I mean it. I thought about how no matter what he thought about, or how hard he thought it, he could not move his legs, thrash his arms, swim a lap. In his case, there is no truth to "mind over matter." The matter is what matters and there's no overcoming it.

In my case, though, the biggest barrier to the swim was my brain, and the heavy sack called fear I hefted over my left shoulder like a bag of rocks.

In the sack of fear, I have carried at one time or another:
the dark,
thunder,
lightning,
earthquakes,
sunburn,
big dogs,
my own sexuality,
other people's sexuality,
being a disappointment,
fireworks,
talking in my sleep,
men,
drunk people,
mean people,
mean dogs,
fast cars,

the loud bang made by popped balloons,
women who know what do with make-up,
(let's face it) most all women,
not being liked (see above entries on women),
athletes,
rats,
motorcycles,
Halloween,
escalators,
running out of bananas,
math,
looking down from the tops of tall things,
looking up at the tops of tall things,
speaking in front of groups,
horror movies,
roller coasters,
spiders.

I have feared that I would
never have a baby,
have a baby and the baby would die,
die in a nuclear holocaust,
live through a nuclear holocaust,
cause pain,
run out of money,
get a lot of money and do something stupid with it,
go crazy,
go crazy and everyone would know but me,
show too much cleavage,
throw up on the plane,
be famous but for something nefarious,
be forgotten,
get an earache,

pee my pants,
never pass my driver's test (third time's the charm!).

I was afraid
that there was no God,
or that there was a God but that
my fundamentalist cousins were right after all
and I had no business being a pastor.

I was afraid of being laughed at.

And these are just the ones that come to mind off the top of my head. Where do they come from, all those fears? I look back, back, back. I can remember the first time I consciously felt afraid. I was maybe five and hiking with my family and some friends in a wild place near our house. It was early spring, but it must have been warm because I had tied the red coat with the white, fur-lined hood around my waist and my blonde hair blew around my head in the little breeze.

The path came to a creek, and we walked across it together on a small dam, holding hands. I looked confidently at the face of the trusted adult friend whose hand I was holding.

"Isn't it neat?"

"Actually, I'm afraid of heights," she answered, "and being up this high makes me scared."

She spoke matter-of-factly, but I heard a tremor in her voice. The water swirled below where we stood on the narrow concrete and I realized it was high—and just like that, I was afraid, too. I wanted to run to safety as fast as I could, but my feet were pinned to the concrete. I was dizzy and faint with the knowledge that adults, who until now had seemed impervious to anything even unpleasant, could actually feel fear.

I don't know how, or if, the rest of my life's fear grew out of that moment. All I know is that for a long time I was afraid a lot. But more often than I was actually afraid, I was afraid of being afraid. So I arranged my life so that I would not have to walk up toward anything that might bring fear. Being married to Jeff, I saw that his life is not so much about fears (although he certainly has those, as you will find if you set a spider down in front of him) but about assessment, about asking before each action, "Do I have it in me?" He's learned to be painfully honest with himself in the answer.

Each time I got in the pool to train for the tri, I realized that this was the fear that I had most of all—that I would not have "it" in me. Jeff has a disability, one he cannot overcome enough to swim, but one he can manage with care and planning and help. I had an impairment that kept me from swimming. Those ears! Those ears! But my impairment was reasonably accommodated. If I had a disability that was keeping me out of the water, it was fear.

In the end, what it took to learn to swim was to look fear in the face. Not fear that I was going to drown (although in truth that was a real possibility given the thrashing—have I mentioned the thrashing?). The real fear was that I would look foolish. This fear may have been the Mother of All Fears, the one that gave birth to all the others, and could be condensed into three small, harmless looking words, "People will laugh."

I heard a story long ago from a guy who in mid-life embraced mediocrity. I remember he said he picked up the tuba, that he played it terribly and with the gusto that comes from having nothing to prove. He knew he was terrible and he also knew that playing the tuba gave him great pleasure. Eventually, he put together a band of others like him, and they played terribly, exuberantly together.

The training and preparation is in the past. This is the day of the triathlon and it's already one third over. It is the end of the first event, and I clamber out of the pool. I am not afraid. I have nothing to prove. I swam like the tuba player blatted—terribly and exuberantly.

The other triathletes by the door are smiling, sure, but they are not laughing at me. Or if they are, I don't care. Since I'm one of them now, I give them a high five as I jog past because I'm pretty sure that's what real triathletes do.

Or is it a fist bump?

Whatever.

part two

RIDE

I I | *In Which I Ride a Bike*

Once I leave the pool, my bare feet slap against the path that leads from the pool across the parking lot. Squinting ahead, I can pick out the little towel I brought from home, lying on the ground next to my bike. Something I read said that it would make me look like an experienced triathlete if I brought a little towel on which to organize my transition gear—in my case, shoes, a fleece headband to cover my ears (the delicate ears! protect them!), my helmet and a little skirt to pull over my suit. There was some confusion about my race number. I first pinned it to my swimsuit, then looking around noticed no one else had it that way. I had taken it off again and left it here on the little towel, too. I pin it on now. I squish my damp feet into bike shoes, clip the helmet under my neck and I am off around the corner and down the hill.

It is a perfect day for biking. The sun is warm but not too hot. I saw on the map that we will make a loop six and half miles or so out, six and half miles or so back. I've been saying "sixandahalfmiles, sixanda-halfmiles" in my head, and studying the wavy line drawn to show the route on the race's website, but I had not reckoned on how rural the route would be. In just a minute, I am past the houses and out of the little town.

My feet go around, my lungs move air in and out, my heart beats. Everything is whizzing past faster than I believe my feet can rotate, but at the same time, I see with unusual clarity individual clouds in an un-naturally blue sky, a field in which something purplish is blooming, the bright green bicycle of a curly haired woman near me. I remember another spring day like this when I learned that I knew how to pray after all in Roberta's office and everything seemed more real than usual. Everything seems more real than usual again and I smile at all of it.

I'm no more of a gearhead than I am an athlete, but even I can see that my sturdy, decade-old Schwinn is not the clunkiest bike in this crowd. I feel a surge of affection for my youngest brother, Jacob. Jacob is a gearhead, and he'd advised me to keep this bicycle instead of trading it in on a newer, no doubt faster, one. He was right. This bike is not a racer, but she will get me where I'm going, no problem.

Oh, yes, my bike. What's wrong with it? Something.

Something's wrong with the brake handle on the right side, which luckily is the one that operates the front brake. The front brakes always seem like extra brakes to me, and I hardly ever use them, except on big hills. The course description said "gently" and "rolling," so I'm not expecting any big hills.

Still, I experimentally pull on the brake handle. Nothing happens at all. I pull it again. With the same strange clarity that I see the colors around me, I know that something is wrong but I don't feel afraid. Which is, you know, strange for me.

My feet go around, my lungs breathe, my heart beats.

If it weren't for the nagging thought that I should probably do something about that brake, I would be perfectly happy.

Up ahead, I see a guy in an orange vest directing us around a corner. "Hey," I call as I whiz by, "do you guys have any bike tools on you?"

"Nope, sorry."

I keep on, braking only with my left hand.

Around a sharpish corner, I head up a steeper hill than I had reckoned on. I begin a little argument in my head with whoever wrote "gently" and "rolling," but then there's no time to think. My lungs strain and burn. I can tell that eventually the left knee is going to give me trouble, but for now I keep spinning. Some strong looking guys are speeding past the other way, looking cool and relaxed on the downhill. They shout encouragement that I can't quite hear, but I think it's something about the turn-around being close.

Purplish green field, yellow flowers in the ditch, brown farmhouse. I squeeze past a red truck that's trying to pass the line of cyclists.

There's no way I'm going to make it back down that hill with only one brake.

What to do? What to do?

I guess the strong guys were saying the turn around was not far after all, because here it is! The woman at this station in an orange vest does not have any bike tools either, but instead of whizzing past, I stop to look at the brake myself. I'm more than half hoping that someone who knows something, or anything, about bicycle repair will stop and help me, but no one does.

Really, it's inexcusable how little I know about the bicycle I'm riding. Why didn't I take that basic repairs class at the bike store? I peer at the front wheel. Even with my extreme lack of bike repair skills, I see what's wrong. There is a metal knob doohickey that should be fixed through a metal loop thingamabob. I wonder if I can fix it myself. I pull on the doohickey and pass it through the thingamabob and it attaches! In the meantime, quite a few cyclists have passed me.

Someone shouts, "Are you OK?"

"I think so!"

I ride in a little circle to make sure the brake is working. I pull it and feel the satisfying tug of a brake engaging.

Many people come to triathlon from running, and runners think of the cycle as the rest period in between the swim and the real event—running—which is to follow.

This makes it easy for a nonathlete on a heavy bike to pass, and on the back side of the loop, I do pass just for fun. At the bottom of that steep hill I had to push to climb earlier, I come up behind a slenderer and younger racer on a lighter bike. I holler "passing" and ding, ding my little bell, which is technically the safe and polite thing to do, but which also is obnoxiously enjoyable. The other racer will pass me easily on the run, obviously, but she won't be able to ring a little bell when she does it.

We round back into town, past the houses and through the park. One. More. Climb. The last hill is only a little less steep than my roof, which I know because I climbed up not long ago to clean the skylight, and then got stuck and had to yell until my husband could wheel over to get a neighbor to help me down.

No one can help me now. I have to get this bike up this hill by myself. I stand and keep pumping and remember a friend's husband who used to advise against walking bikes up hills back in Seattle. "Either way, you gotta get the bike up the hill. Might as well ride it," he used to say.

I hear a sound like "grrrrummmmmmphhhhgghhh!" and realize the sound is me, grumphing with effort. My left knee is definitely going to be an issue. It's both stabbing and throbbing, but I hardly notice. I'm ecstatic because all around me athletes, real ones, are jumping off to walk their bikes. But, egged on by some enthusiastic little boys standing on the top of the hill shouting, "Come on! You can do it!" I ride my bike all the way to the top.

12 | *Bikes, I've Known a Few*

I rode on a bike for a while before I ever pedaled a bike. When I was small, my mom settled me in the bike seat on the back of her dark brown ten-speed and puffed me up the rolling, sandy back roads of northern Wisconsin as cars whizzed by.

You'd never be able to buy a bike seat like that now. The seat may have had a seat belt or strap, but if it did, I don't remember it. We never used seat belts anyway, not even in cars. What I remember are black metal armrests that dug into my sides as we swayed up a hill, a hard little back that I tried not to lean on, and the conviction that if I did not remain perfectly still, we would both tumble over. I would not call the experience enjoyable, exactly, but there was a certain breathless thrill about it that I still capture from time to time on a bicycle.

I received my own first bike on one of those moments that I only realized much later must have been a big challenge for my young parents. The Christmas I was five, I ran down the wooden steps of the big old house we were renting to find a yellow (as requested) bike with a banana seat (as requested) resting on its kickstand (as requested!) under the tree. Does it seem ungrateful to say that even with all those requests granted, I still wished the banana seat had flowers on it, that the handles had streamers, well, streaming out like the bikes of the girls next door?

I loved that bike, which I learned to ride indoors that Wisconsin winter, wobbling back and forth between the living room and the kitchen. The next spring, I took off down the sidewalk, still wobbly but really riding all on my own.

A couple of years later, on a family ride, I skidded on a patch of gravel and flew, landing on hands and knees by the side of the road. There was a lot of crying and shaking of my head, while my dad tried to urge me back on the bike. An unknown couple came by, the sweaters slung casually over their shoulders marking them immediately. Summer people.

"Is the little girl all right?"

"Fine, fine, everything's fine . . . ," my dad sang the chorus of my childhood.

I don't remember the rest of that day, but my dad says he bullied me back onto the bike and back home. I was not a determined child, but after that, I made up my mind that bikes were not for me.

We must have gotten rid of it in a move because I don't remember the yellow banana bike at all after that. Sometimes I would tip around the yard on my mom's old brown ten-speed, the perilous kid's seat I'd ridden in so long ago still rusting on the back. I never took that bike very far, though. I didn't really want to. Riding bikes any distance seemed like another thing that adults had figured out, that maybe I would just know how to do when I got older.

One family friend, Susan Dexter, rode a moped—the first one I had ever seen. Besides riding a moped, Susan painted moody, gorgeous paintings of leaves and flowers. She sang in the choir of the little church my dad pastored, and every Christmas Eve warbled and trilled through the solo of "O Holy Night," a performance that I am sorry to say that my brother Mark and I imitated all year around. But even though we laughed, we loved her.

Somehow Susan Dexter got the idea that I should receive elocution lessons, an old fashioned idea even in that old-fashioned time and place. I would get dropped off at her place out in the woods, and she would drink something amber out of a little glass and lead me in reciting her favorite poets.

Once upon a midnight drrrrreary,
While I pondered weak and wearrry,
Over many a quaint and currrrrious
Volume of forgotten llllllore.

She would begin, rolling her rrrs and llls, and I imitated her as best as I could, my ten-year-old tongue struggling to repeat Edgar Allen Poe's beautiful melancholy words, to roll my rrrs and llls as splendidly as she did.

I do not remember Susan Dexter (who we always called by her whole name to distinguish her from the other Susan, the one with the long red hair) driving a car, although she must have done so, especially in winter. What I remember is the moped, which was not a tiny motorcycle like the things that are called mopeds now. Susan Dexter's moped was a bicycle with a small motor bolted on the support bar that would kick in when she had pumped her feet fast enough. Her skirt flapped in the breeze and her little helmet shone as she buzzed around the island.

One Sunday morning, she greeted me at the church door with her usual wild grin.

"Look what happened to me this morning!" she trilled daintily, raising her skirt up to her thighs to reveal two skinned knees.

"The moped went rrrrright into the ditch."

The shock of old lady knees, the stream of blood and even a glimpse of old lady knickers were a potent anti-incentive to a nervous little girl who hardly needed a reason to never ride bikes. Susan Dexter kept buzzing around on her moped even after her tumble that Sunday morning, but after that, I really had no interest in riding a bike.

My disinterest lasted until college, when the boyfriend I wanted to marry got me one as a courtship gift. It was huge and heavy with three gears, tires as wide as my wrist and a flowery, straw basket wired in the front. When I rode it around campus, I felt so invincible that I would hum the Wicked Witch of the West song from *The Wizard of Oz*. Ditty-oot-do-do-dooooo-do, Ditty-oot-do-do-dooooo-do. I felt as certain that I would never fall off that bike as I felt about my future with the boyfriend. But the bike got stolen. The boyfriend left.

The boyfriend left. Seems like such a small sentence now but, oh goodness, those small words contain so much big misery. The boyfriend lived for a while in a big house with a bunch of other college friends. They called the house the Yellow House, reasonably enough because that was its color. A couple of friends and I who had all been dumped at one time or another by a guy in the house called it the House of Ex-Boyfriends, like that was their whole identity. Being an ex-girlfriend was certainly my identity for a long time after that, and I went about it messily, with copious tears and snot.

One night, my brother Mark called me from his college town, a state away.

"What are you doing?" he asked.

"Just lying on the floor, listening to Patsy Cline." I sniffled into the phone, with "I Fall to Pieces" blaring in the background.

"Well, stop it. Get up and go do something else."

For a long time, getting up and doing something else did not seem possible. But after time, what seemed like a long time, measured more in years than in months, I was able to say it without doubling over in pain. The boy was gone.

The boy was really gone, but my new love of bikes stayed. I graduated from college, picked up another bike somewhere, and used it to commute the mile or so to my job at a health food store. One time, I arrived crying for my mid-afternoon shift.

A group of college guys had yelled at me out of the car window, "You're uglier than my dog's butt!"

When the store manager asked me what was wrong, and I told him, he looked incredulous.

"But, but, but, that's not even *true*," he sputtered.

It took years before I would believe all the time that just because someone said it (my parents, my boyfriends, my roommates, some random asshats driving by in a car) it did not make it true. Even before I believed "just because they say it doesn't make it true" all of the time, I knew it while I was riding my bike. Biking meant freedom and wind in my hair and strong legs going around.

Biking also meant being out there for all to see, meant being made aware of my deficiencies, including an ugliness so pronounced, according to those college guys, that it was worth noting out an open car window. Usually that was the kind of thing that would stop me in my tracks, make me stop, lean the bike against a shed, and give it up. But even though I chafed against the words, they did not stop me. I kept on riding.

That was the only time someone said something quite so mean to me. But if you're on a bike, people will feel they can talk to you or yell at you as they speed past.

Years later, I moved across country to Seattle in the rainy middle of winter. I had no job to speak of, no car, and no friends in town except for my new boyfriend, who worked all day. I spent a lot of that winter tooling around on my bike, exploring the city. One time on the Burke-Gilman trail, another cyclist came up next to me and somehow we started talking. He was so cool that I hope you'll know what I mean when I say that he looked more like a biker than a cyclist. His long beard flapped in the wind and his tattoos glistened in the rain.

I think he was the one who advised me to get toe clips so that the power of my pedaling could work when my legs were going up as well as when they were heading down. He ended the conversation by saying "... and get some real shoes!" before he zoomed off. I glanced down at my deeply uncool blue high tops. "But, I'm having so much fun!" I should have shouted after him. Instead, I kept cycling, wiping the winter rain out my eyes. I didn't have a bike light then, or a cool jersey, or (evidently) even the right shoes. My bike was old and heavy. But that didn't stop me from riding in the rain, from loving the coast downhill, and from laughing at the water squishing under my wheels in the puddle that formed at the bottom. I kept pumping my legs and I kept going. Round and round and round.

THE BREATH JOURNALS: PART IV

When I was in college, I was trying to impress a guy. There was a lot of that in those days, but this guy really was adorable and deserved much better than I was able to give him, considering I was still pining for Mr. House of Ex-Boyfriends. Anyway, I was trying, so I joined his martial arts class. This was in Scotland, where I was studying for a semester, and the teacher was a former member of the British Navy. The teacher saw through my motives right away, so he did not bother much with me. But he really was serious about teaching the young men in the class. He would kick them ungently in the ribs as he prowled around the classroom.

"Breathe," he'd growl. "If you don't breathe, you die."

I didn't learn a lot of martial arts in that class, but I sure learned what would happen if you didn't breathe. You'd die. Or at least get a toe to the solar plexus.

13 | *Easy Is Hard. And Vice Versa*

I never was a cool cyclist in cool Seattle, even when I got a little more gear. But I knew I could keep going if I just kept moving my legs, up and down, around and around. I do not always know, in fact, when to stop. It's taken me a long time to realize that moving is mindless, easy for me. It's resting that's hard, that takes work.

In her heartening book *Sabbath in the Suburbs*, MaryAnn McKibben-Dana intersperses her narrative about keeping Sabbath with her young family with "Sabbath Hacks." A hack, in this case, is like a computer shortcut. In other words, a hack is not exactly the kosher way to get something done, but it's often easier or faster or just plain better than the usual way. One of her hacks is to remember that the harder thing is sometimes the easier thing. Dana gives this example from her own family.

> Every few months, Robert and I get into serious laziness with going to the grocery store. Robert won't feel like making a list, or I won't feel like going except to buy the stopgap supplies: milk and bread. When faced with the decision between shopping or sitting on the couch, the couch always wins. The problem is that the easier thing (couch) takes a lot more effort in the long run. We spend days or weeks limping along on crappy fast food and mystery freezer containers crusted over with ice. Life would be so much better if we just up and went to the dang store. The harder thing (getting off our duffs and shopping) becomes easier (better meal options, happier family).[5]

---

5. MaryAnn McKibben-Dana, *Sabbath in the Suburbs* (Atlanta: Chalice Press, 2012), 121.

"You can be as gracious as you want about it, but your life is just harder than other people's," my mom tells me long distance.

"Um, I guess so," I reply into the phone.

I don't really know what to say. My life doesn't seem that hard to me. Once a guy biked up to me in the rain and kindly, but firmly, let me know that my gear was not at all cool. But I'm having so much fun! I wanted to shout at him as he whipped past me. It was too late. He was in the fast lane and already gone. It's like that now. I keep pumping my legs up and down, up and down. I will keep moving. And sometimes, I even get to coast on the downhill. I don't know how to show other people the joy of that—or if I even should.

My mom is not the only one to tell me that my life with a disabled husband seems hard. I've talked to many people for whom nothing seems harder than being in a wheelchair. To most people, a wheelchair means confinement, stigma, difficulty. I've known people who have given up activities they love—going to church, getting their hair done, seeing friends—because their legs are no longer reliable, but they refuse to use a wheelchair. People have told me they would rather be dead than use a wheelchair.

I have to be patient when I encounter this attitude because for Jeff and me, the opposite is true. For us, what seems like the harder thing (wheelchair) is really the easier thing (freedom, sociability, independence). Without it, Jeff would be stuck in . . . well, I don't even know where. Without it, Jeff would just be stuck.

Jeff's disease, spinal muscular atrophy, is progressive. When you or I use our muscles to the point of exhaustion (assuming that the "you" in this case does not have muscular dystrophy, too!) our muscles break down but they build back up again. Jeff's DNA is missing a piece, so his muscles break down but do not build back up. That means that he started out childhood being able to do many things that other kids did—go bowling, slide down snowy hills, even run through the neighborhood on those twilight games of chase he remembers with great fondness. But instead of getting stronger like the other kids, Jeff kept getting weaker.

As a kid, I never really thought about walking. I just put one foot in front of the other and did it. Jeff had to think about walking every minute of every day. He remembers what it was like in his late teens to have every decision be based on his inability to walk far. He would hide out in the stairwell at school, hoping no one would catch him dodging the fire drill.

A fall off a bike for me meant never trying again so I would never fall again. A fall for Susan Dexter meant a couple of skinned knees and a joke. A fall for Jeff meant lying on his back until someone had enough compassion and strength to help him up, meant it was time to start using a wheelchair. Which he did at age seventeen.

At that time, and for the first years we were together, Jeff used a three-wheel scooter to get around. These are the kind of devices they rent in Vegas to fat gamblers who can't be troubled to walk all the way from Caesar's Palace to Treasure Island. To the average eye, the scooter doesn't seem like a serious wheelchair. It seems like the kind of device you could jump out of any minute you felt like it.

In the early days of our marriage, waiters in crowded restaurants sometimes looked at Jeff, then looked at the scooter, then at the tables.

"Can you get out of that thing?" they asked.

The answer was no, but it pleased Jeff in those days to look like the kind of guy who could choose to stand up and walk to the table at any moment. We didn't really realize it at the time, but the harder thing seemed like the easier thing. It seemed like the easier thing not to seem too disabled, to give the impression that he could jump up at any minute and be on his way. It seemed like an easier thing to avoid the open pity, the less open scorn, the "I-would-rather-be-dead" hidden behind the smile of even the most polite passerby.

However, there were many problems with the scooter. It was no good at all on any bumpy or uneven surface, it was bulky, and worst of all it did not support Jeff's back, so as he got weaker his scoliosis (a secondary condition experienced by many people with MD) got more pronounced. Also, as he slumped over, pressure sores started to pop up on his skin from the unevenness of his weight and the inadequacy of the cushion.

If you don't live mostly in a wheelchair or a bed, you probably get little scrapes and bruises from time to time. These little scrapes heal, get better. But if you're sitting or lying on the sore all day and if you can't shift your weight very well and there's not very good circulation anyway, a pressure sore can move from a minor annoyance to a major health problem extremely quickly.

Look, I could tell you more, but then I would have to write a whole 'nother book. It would be very long and it would be called Pressure Sores We Have Known. If you want to gross yourself out, you can go ahead and Google "pressure sores." If you do, make sure to click the images tab.

Go ahead. I'll wait.

Or just take my word for it when I tell you that a pressure sore to a disabled person can become all-consuming, debilitating, and even— although not as yet, thank goodness, in Jeff's case—fatal.

Still, in spite of these problems, the scooter was familiar. And familiarity is very often the harder thing that seems like the easier thing. Finally his scooter gave up the ghost, and Jeff got a new wheelchair for most of the time. The new wheelchair, the iBot, supported his back better, went easily on grass and up curbs and even had a function that allowed him to go up and down stairs. The iBot was the easier thing in many ways, but Jeff continued to use the scooter around the house because he could get independently in and out of the bathroom in it.

I thought I was visible and vulnerable on my bike, but that's nothing compared to Jeff when he's out in the iBot. The iBot was invented by Dean Kaman, the same guy who invented the two-wheeled Segways now used primarily by meter readers and tourists. The iBot runs on the same principles as the Segway, kept upright by gyroscopes. The iBot can run on four wheels like a regular wheelchair, but it can also balance on two wheels. It looks more like a circus trick than an assistive device the first time you see it. It always draws a crowd.

Jeff especially drew a crowd the last day we used the stair function. Going up and down stairs in an iBot is possible but requires an assistant (that would be me) to perform a heart-stopping maneuver that feels a lot like pushing the wheelchair user down the stairs. The assistant grasps the iBot by the back bar, tips the chair way back and then all the way forward again, while the wheelchair makes a steam-punky-sounding wheeze of hydraulics and gently clicking moving parts.

At least, that's how it's supposed to work. On the way to watch our son skate in an inaccessible ice rink one New Year's Day, distracted by the friendly guy who had a million questions and a bad sense of personal space, I froze mid-stairwell and so did the chair. I remember the sun shining brightly on the short flight of steps that seemed like a mountain. I lay Jeff on his back, still in the wheelchair. And he hung out right there on the steps until a group of tipsy hockey players poured out of the bar next door to the rink and helped me get him up.

See, all that seems hard. I guess it was in its way. After that I did put my foot down about my unwillingness to perform the stair function ever again. But, if you are going to fall, the best place to do it is in front of a bar where a bunch of affable hockey players are drinking off their New Year's Eve hangover. And the best time to do it is on one of those rare Pacific Northwest days when the watery sun is peering through the clouds for once. And the best way is to be laid down on your back, still in your chair, so no one gets hurt.

14 | *Falling Down, Literally and Not So Literally*

There are so many ways to fall. Here's another one:

We talk about it differently, that October day. I call it "the day I dropped you." Jeff has always insisted that I am not to blame and calls it "the day the belt broke." Whatever you call it, it was a day when the wheels stopped moving easily around. A day we had to set a new course.

The thing about those days that change everything is that they are never the ones you think they are going to be, not the ones you plan for. Here's an example. Jeff did not plan to ever be a father. With his disability, he could not imagine it. But I wanted nothing else, and after we were married I wheedled him mercilessly. One day at work, headphones blocking out the chaos of the open office around him, Jeff heard a rock version of the song "Three Is a Magic Number" (from the popular 1970s–1980s children's TV show *Schoolhouse Rock*) He started to cry on "a man and a woman had a little baby."

> A man and a woman had a little baby
> Yeah, they did
> And there were three in the family
> And that's a magic number[6]

By the end of the song, he called me and said, "Yes. Let's do it."

When he got home we kissed and laughed and cried and laughed some more. Then we neglected the diaphragm for one giggly weekend, and in the due course of time, we two were three.

I did not know that it would not be pregnancy, nor Elijah's birth, nor the short nights and long days to follow that changed me. I really changed, heart and soul, ten months later. While the baby and I looked at a poster of a mother and baby polar bear in his room, he threw his little arms into me in imitation of the bears' embrace, grinned at me, and said, "Awwww." It was not my son's birth, but his first moment of spontaneous affection that broke my heart unexpectedly, completely, and finally wide open.

So it was, years after the baby was grown, that the moment that changed everything for Jeff and me was not anything we planned. It was

---

6. Bob Dorough, "Three Is a Magic Number," © 1973, written for the ABC TV series *Schoolhouse Rock*, Rhino Records.

a precarious business in those days, getting him out of bed. Even though we knew on some level that it wasn't that safe, it was what we had always done, so we kept doing it. The harder thing seemed like the easier thing.

Before that day, I was the only one who would lift him out of bed. We hired personal care attendants to assist with other things, but it was only me who would clip a wide belt around Jeff's hips, clamp his knees between my knees, help him to lean forward so his head and shoulders were leaning into my left hip, and then, grabbing the belt, swing him around to be seated in the chair of his scooter. From there, he was able to move around in the bathroom, perform a shuffling transfer from toilet seat and back to scooter, from scooter to shower bench, from shower bench back to scooter. He would emerge from the bathroom two hours later, exhausted already from the effort of getting from place to place, but triumphant. He had done it. He had taken care of himself for another day.

This October day was like any other day. I helped him sit precariously on the side of the bed. I slid the belt under his hips, clamped it closed and caught his knees between my knees. I turned to shift him into the chair and the belt gave way. Jeff collapsed to the floor in terrible slow motion, screaming and swearing. I tried to grab him under the armpits, but his dead weight was too much for me. In the end, I had to let go.

The rest of the day is like a series of snapshots, intense memories unconnected to each other. I remember covering him with a blanket, calling our helper, who was washing dishes in the next room. I remember apologizing and Jeff managing through clenched, chattering teeth to assure me for the first of several thousand times that this was not my fault. I remember that somehow the two of us lifted Jeff onto the toilet.

I remember making a few gasping sobs and our helper patting me sympathetically, "I've never heard a sound like the sound Jeff made when he fell."

I remember being glad that Elijah wasn't home to hear that sound. I remember calling someone at the church to cancel my meetings and Bible study that day. I do not remember getting Jeff dressed, although we must have, and I do not remember getting to the hospital. I do remember watching the clock as both breakfast and lunchtime passed by in the ER. I remember that I didn't want to leave to eat because the doctor might arrive at any moment to give us a prognosis.

Mostly I remember thinking that Jeff's fall had to change things and being frightened of the uncertainty that came with that change. And knowing that no matter how frightened and uncertain I was, Jeff was a thousand times more so. When I fell off my bike all those years ago, I made a choice. I crossed my arms and shook my head and said, "No more biking." When Susan Dexter fell off her moped, she shook it off with a grin and a trill.

Jeff does not have the luxury of choice, of shaking it off. If we couldn't do the transfer anymore, how would he get out of bed? Use the toilet? Take a shower? What would we do?

Well, that long afternoon in the ER while we waited for Jeff to get casts and pain medications, it seemed impossible. It wasn't impossible, though. It took time, but we figured out a new way. I *want* to say that Jeff was always gracious, and that I was always patient, in the healing weeks that followed the fall. Jeff continued to maintain that it was not my fault, but sometimes he snapped at me about little things, sometimes I got defensive and histrionic.

For example: Imagine us in the bathroom, maybe ten days after the fall. Imagine me pushing Jeff in his wheeled bath chair from the sink into the shower. Imagine that maybe I take a corner too quickly. Then listen.

"Be careful!" he shouts. "Think about my feet."

I cry immediately, the kind of tears for which the phrase "she burst into" was invented. "It hurts my feelings you would even think that," I sob. "I don't think about anything but your feet."

Slowly and painfully the breaks and sprains in Jeff's feet healed. A change was made—we stopped doing the belt transfer and started doing a transfer with a lift. It did not happen the next day, or the day after that, but after a time we got a mechanical lift, one that the paid helpers also could operate.

Getting a mechanical lift seemed like the harder thing. It took up precious floor space in our tiny ranch house bedroom. As many steps as the belt transfer required, moving around in the lift used even more. But the biggest hard thing about the lift was that it was a daily reminder to Jeff and to me that Jeff was really, truly disabled.

You might think that, what with the wheelchair and all, we would have figured this out by now. When we were first married, we went for genetic counseling so we could make an informed decision about whether to have children. Since Jeff has SMA, we knew that any child born of our union would also be a carrier. He wanted me to get tested. If I was an unknown carrier, the chance would be one in four that any children born of our union would also manifest symptoms. We wanted to know our chances before we started trying to have children of our own. We went into the university hospital in Seattle, where we were living at the time, and both got tested.

Jeff had been treated at the Mayo Clinic for SMA since his childhood, so we already knew that he had the condition. We were mostly there to see about me. The genetic counseling student who met with us after the test entered the room gravely. Ignoring me, she looked sadly at my husband, seated in his wheelchair.

"I'm sorry to inform you, you have muscular dystrophy," she whispered. Both Jeff and I laughed out loud then (I mean, obviously!) and many times afterward. If he was having a particularly trying day, we could sometimes crack each other up by whispering somberly, "Did you know, you are disabled? I'm sorry to break it to you . . ."

Jeff has the disability you can see. But the truth is that neither he nor I comfortably inhabit the bodies we have been given. Mostly, though, we don't think about it unless (or until) we absolutely have to.

Sure, he was disabled, we could allow ourselves to think before the mechanical lift brought its irrefutable evidence into our bedroom. Sure, he was disabled, but not that disabled. He could move around in the bathroom by himself, after all, and no matter how taxing it was, that counted for something.

Although the mechanical lift seemed like the harder thing for all these reasons, really and truly it was the easier thing. Easier on my back and knees for one thing. And easier on my mind and my perceived ability to take risks. It was after the mechanical lift that I was able to consider training for the tri because our life was not wholly dependent on my strong back and legs. It was easier on Jeff's body in ways I probably could not even know. The wheels, I began to realize, had not stopped after all. They were just carrying us down a new and unfamiliar road.

Jeff will fall again. Now that I think about it, I will, too, probably. So will you, one way or another. Sometimes he and I and you will respond to those falls with grace and sometimes with rage. Sometimes he and I and you will respond with patience and sometimes with frustration. Sometimes things will be just the way they were before, sometimes they will be harder and sometimes they will be much, much easier.

Like my dad, I used to always want to say to everyone, all the time, that everything would be fine, fine, fine. My dad and I have both grown up, though, and we talk sometimes about knowing now what we didn't used to know, including that "everything-is-fine" is not, as we so long thought, what keeps the wheels moving smoothly along the road. Truth does.

"Every day and every way things are getting better and better" was a slogan of psychologist and pharmacist Emile Coue. He was French, but his words have sunk deep into my American bones. It's not just about things, though. People are supposed to get better and better, too. When they don't, it makes us jump in to offer miracle cures or platitudes or alternatively makes us want to turn away from the shame of witnessing what we cannot fix.

When I was first with Jeff, I kept waiting for him to get better. Every day and every way. The thing is, though, he won't. He'll keep getting weaker and weaker every day of his life. Being able to say that out loud is one of the hardest things I've ever done; it's also the one that has made me strongest and, in the end, happiest. I used to think happy lies made people happy. But knowing the truth, and finding the joy anyway, makes that joy fiercer and more precious than I think most people understand.

Since those days when I whispered to a spiritual director that I could not pray at all, I've become a sort of professional pray-er. I pray out loud at hospital beds and in nursing homes and on living room couches. I pray to begin meetings and to end them. I pray because we need a break from our regular way of thinking and doing. I pray because I believe that God hears our prayers—even if I don't understand how that works. I pray when everything is not fine and nothing can be fixed and no one is getting better. I pray in those times for patience, for courage, for strength.

I try to be truthful in my prayers, to show God's work to other people the way Jan and Roberta and other wise women have shown it to me. One time, I offered to pray with a pal over the phone when she called, upset.

"God," I started, having heard a litany of frustrations and not really knowing where to begin. "Well, sometimes things just suck and we don't know why."

If my prayer offered answers or words of encouragement, neither of us remembers now. It was the willingness to say that things sometimes just suck that she appreciated. They don't sound like hopeful words, but they are.

Because it give us hope in other people when they can see us as we are, and meet us there, not try to make us something else. It is the best prayer of all to name things not as we wish they would be, but exactly as they are, to let our pains and sorrows ride on swift wheels out to God.

15 | *Tri Training, Marriage, and a Girl Called Ruth*

Several times a week, all through the wet early winter of 2012, I left the house for a training ride. On very rainy or cold days, I drove to the rec center and rode the stationary bike there. But since I could read a magazine while I was doing it, it didn't seem sufficiently rigorous. Actually, at first even biking outside didn't seem all that rigorous. An easy push, push, push, and then a coast. I moved my legs around a while, then I started out riding around the neighborhood. I looped around the wet pavement by the fake little lake a few blocks away, pedaling fast only long enough to get around the geese. Did I mention geese in my list of fears? I guess not, but the geese in this particular park have a vicious disregard for other creatures, which makes me think that they must think they are at the top of the food chain. Anyway, the geese always hang out on the south side of the lake, so I could coast around the north side.

I never saw anyone else anywhere near my age biking around the lake. It was mostly little kids with training wheels, biting their lips in concentration and smiling with pride and awe at me on my big bike. Or slighter bigger kids carrying backpacks and who, if they looked at me at all, had the exact opposite of pride or awe on their faces. It did not take too long at all to graduate from the path around the lake.

Portland is a biking town. And although we live a little ways out of town, in the first tier of suburbs, there are many biking lanes and paths not far from my house, so I tried some of those.

"Careful," a seasoned cyclist at my church warned me, "don't get going so fast that you run into one of those posts they put in the middle of the paths to keep cars off."

It seemed impossible that I would ever bike that fast or that mindlessly in those first weeks of training. Biking for me in those days was all about, you know, the coasting. The path I rode most often winds sweetly through parks and little wetlands, around and behind a row of townhouses. I started training for the tri in December, and the pavement is always wet in winter in Oregon, even on sunny days. I was careful not to fall.

After some time, I pedaled faster, rode further, looked for a route that would loop around on streets as well as the little paths. One rainy cold day, I caught a piece of glass in my wheel at a place where the path crossed a busy road (a highway really). The air wheezed out slowly until the rim was flat on the road and I had to stop.

I did not have a spare, and even if I had, I would not have known how to change it. According to the tracker app thingy that Jeff had put on my phone, I was 7.3 miles from home, too far to walk. And even if I could have walked, what would I have done with my bike? I had no lock. I stuck my head in the tiny store they sometimes put there on the island in the middle of the gas station, which would be useful in a real pinch only if you could live on either cigarettes or chewing gum. If I expected help from the gas station guys, I didn't exactly get it. So I cried for few minutes, which in those days was my default response to most any emotion. Then I called Jeff (who was about a quarter of the way through a two-and-half-hour getting-up routine so couldn't offer more than sympathy, which he did) and then my best friend, who didn't pick up. Finally I called a retired guy from church who I knew had a station wagon, and he came and got me.

As incidents go, it really wasn't all that serious. No one was hurt, including the Schwinn; it only took three calls to get help, and it wasn't even raining. But I realized that day that if I were going to do this sprint triathlon thing, it was going to be up to me to figure it out. Even if figuring it out only meant calling as many people as I could until I got the help I needed.

When my aunt had first heard about my relationship with Jeff, she laughed, not unkindly. "You always have to do the hard thing, huh?"

Since she was laughing, I probably did, too, because I'm usually like that, but inside I bristled a little.

One of my first real jobs was for a publishing company. I did a project about peacemaking where a colleague and I traveled to schools and libraries and bookstores around the country. One time a bookstore owner stepped out on the sidewalk and scolded my colleague for taking a smoke break. He was not on her property and there were no children present, but the store owner felt he should not be smoking at all.

"It's so inconsistent with your message of peace," she said.

It had been a long day and I knew my colleague was tired.

"That's right, I smoke. My issue is right out there," he retorted, "What's your issue? The one that you can keep hidden?"

Other marriages, I imagine, have issues that they can keep hidden. In other marriages, couples hoard *Playboy*s or Superman action figures or measuring cups; enjoy secret addictions to caffeine or chips or cigarettes; spend more money than they have on jewelry or online poker or television evangelists.

In one family, a spouse is careful to punch where it won't leave a bruise; in another, a partner withholds sex for an imagined slight; in a third, both kick the dog when the other isn't looking. In one marriage, the couple makes love twice a year; in another, twice a day; in a third, never.

Some spouses give each other the silent treatment for years at a time or never speak without shouting or communicate only to ask, "Pass the potatoes?" One couple talks all the time, but can never tell the truth about the red shoes or the pineapple-upside-down cake incident or the cancer. In other marriages, I imagine serial infidelity, chronic unemployment, a forty-seven-year-old disagreement over blanket sharing that began in the honeymoon suite.

No one need ever know any of these things.

It is not that way in my marriage. As soon as we leave the house, the secret is out. We are rolling along, visible and available for comment for anyone who wants to shout at us as they whiz past, "Issue alert! Guy in wheelchair!"

No stranger looking at us has ever thought, "Wow, it must be so hard not be able to share breakfast."

And yet, Jeff's distaste for the best meal of the day caused more tears in the beginning than his disability. Our first Christmas together, I whipped up a batch of my dad's Swedish pancakes, then cooked and ate them all sobbing while Jeff slept unaware.

Jeff isn't always unaware. Later in our marriage, I realized how ill equipped I was to parent a toddler. I had a headache all the time and I was about to finish graduate school with no real plan about what would happen in the future. I realized this, unfortunately, as I was stepping out of the bathtub. I sat down on the slippery edge of the tub wrapped in a towel, which is where Jeff found me.

"I just feel so unconnected, like I'm drifting. I feel so lonely," I cried.

With a wealth of friends and family, it seemed ungrateful as well as untrue to claim loneliness, but there it was. I wanted to outrun it, outgrow it, this feeling that I was a balloon on a string, floating out of reach of others. If I couldn't outgrow it, I wanted to at least be able to hide it better. Loneliness made me cry and thrash and spend too much money trying to fill the hole it made in my heart. It made me reject people who could have loved me because I was afraid to get hurt. It seemed like the least attractive part of me, the persistence of loneliness in a full life.

"Honey, look at me." He touched my cheek. "I love your loneliness. Other people love your loneliness. It's because of it that you keep reaching out. People are drawn to you because they see it in you and they know you understand them."

When I was a little girl, I got to attend a wedding my dad performed at the little church next door. It made a big impression on me, not least because at the reception the wedding party wheeled out a tandem bike covered with daisies and sang cornily, "Daisy, Daisy, give me your answer true. I'm half crazy all for the love of you. It won't be a stylish marriage. I can't afford a carriage, but you'll look sweet upon the seat of a bicycle built for two." The bride and groom blushed and laughed out loud and then (I can't quite remember this part) either jumped or were pushed into the cold Lake Superior waters.

I guess I imagined that weddings were like marriages. So marriages must be full of singing and goofballery and hope. I imagined happily pedaling off into the sunset on the back of a bike someone else was steering. But I brought myself to marriage—laughing sometimes, sure, but also crying and cringing sometimes. And instead of riding on the back of someone else's bike, I was steering my own. What I had to remember to do was look over and see that someone was wheeling right next to me.

Until I met Jeff, I never had met someone who named loneliness as one of my attractive and beloved qualities. That he loves me because of, not in spite of, the parts of myself I would like to keep hidden is only one of the many things I love about him. His steady confidence in the lovability of my most broken places is one of the many things that keeps the wheels going around and around.

We didn't start out in love. We were friends before we were lovers. Long before Jeff and I were a couple, he was married to someone else and I was in a serious relationship. Years before we moved to the West Coast, we worked together in a small office in northern Minnesota. As work friends, we heated up our ramen noodles and talked. When his first marriage ended, he confided in me that he didn't know how to tell his parents. I asked for his advice about how to decorate a bathroom. We shared small jokes that we can still tell in shorthand like "The elevator!" And night after night, he appeared in my dreams, free from his wheelchair and always running, running, running toward me.

In those early days of friendship, long before I knew he would be the one to ride beside me for life, I talked about him behind his back, with our co-worker Heather. "What do you think about Jeff? Do you think he can, you know, do it?"

"Well, he is married, you know." Heather was much more practical than I.

"I know, I know. But what do you think he can *do?*"

Heather was not much of a giggler, but I was, and just the question thrilled me into giggles. As questions go, it wasn't much to base a relationship on, but it was a start. One question led to another and another and another, both literally and figuratively. Jeff's marriage ended, and so did our jobs at the small publishing house. He boomeranged back to live with his parents for a while and then a friend called from way out in Seattle, promising that intoxicating Western mixed cocktail of freedom and opportunity. Although none of his five brothers or sisters had moved more than a couple of states away at that point, Jeff decided to give it a try. He told me his plans over what we figured would be our last lunch together.

"I'm sorry you're leaving." Our eyes met.

"If only . . . ," he replied, the rest of the sentence fading into regret and lost chance.

We hugged and said goodbye and drove in separate cars to our separate homes in separate cities. He went home to pack; I went home to settle into my life at last. Was it coincidence, then, that a few weeks later, the first day of a road trip to meet my baby brother Noah's new baby in California fell on the same day as Jeff's big move west? Was it coincidence we decided to travel together?

I climbed into his red van that day not thinking of destiny or of coincidence but how I could help Jeff. It was he who helped me. I told him a few secrets by Iowa. By Nebraska, while millions of sandhill cranes streamed across the sky and we drove into what seemed an endless sunset, we were in love.

That's how I tell the story when someone asks me how we met, how we fell in love. But that story doesn't include the hours and weeks and months that followed while I clumsily extricated myself from another relationship, and Jeff settled into a new job. The story doesn't count the pages of letters, log the hours of phone time. And the story does not include the agonizing decision. Would I throw my lot in with Jeff or would I stay in my hometown?

The story of the van ride across Nebraska, the one where we fell in love to the cries of birds and the wild colors of the setting sun does not include the part about selling just about everything I owned to pay for the move. It does not include the story of me pinned to the bed dizzy with fear the January day I was to fly away, while my mom and three brothers stood around me telling me to get up, get up, get *up* while my dad cooked one last breakfast. It does not tell the story of those first days together in a new city.

Those first days were such a mingling of grief and hope and fear and desire. Early on, we took a day trip on a ferry, the quintessential romantic Seattle experience. When we got on the boat, other cars parked all around us, including in front of Jeff's van door. It would have been too cold for Jeff to get out anyway, but the fact that he could not get out even if he'd wanted to was brought home like a knife blade to the gut that day. I started to cry on the ferry and cried the whole day, the whole of the romantic drive up the peninsula and back. Jeff, wisely, did not say much that day. As we rode around (was it tears or rain blurring those trees?), the reality sunk in that life with Jeff would mean so much more than I had thought. It would mean stuckness and joy and apartness and safety and love. I looked at Jeff, wheeling along side me, and realized I wanted not just the fairy-tale marriage, but the whole of it, whatever that would mean.

On an uncharacteristically sunny October day, we were married. We bought groceries and ate them. We laughed some and cried some. We moved from a small apartment to a slightly less small apartment. We made love. We made friends. We argued over his video games and my mania for rearranging furniture. We overdrafted our checking account. We walked under the pine trees to the lake in the city park nearby. We joined a church. We took the bus. We bought a van, and then another when the first one got totaled. We watched lots of old Star Trek. We listened to each other complain about work (his) or school (mine); we held hands. We emptied the cat box. We studied the Bible with a group we found by chance. We protested the sanctions in Iraq and the World Trade Organization. We took each other to movies. We tried to tell the truth and (when we sometimes failed) we tried again. We taught each other how to stay married by just doing it. After a few years, a few hundred discussions, and the few days eschewing a diaphragm, our son was born. We kept doing the same things, only on less sleep.

The days before my marriage, I did not imagine the mundane would bring any satisfaction. I wanted excitement, drama, romance. I wanted to drive west forever into a setting sun while a million white birds fluttered and called overhead. I did not want anything to be ordinary.

Which is why I wanted to change my name from Jennifer (remember all those Jennifers?). My name seemed so pedestrian, so silly, so small. I wanted instead to be called a name that reflected the seriousness and importance of the big life I was to lead. I wanted to change my name to . . . Ruth.

OK, listen. Hold on. Before you tell me that one about the cranky great-aunt Ruth who scared you as a child (and it turns out most everyone has one), let me tell you the story about the original Ruth, the one I wanted to be.

Ruth was married to a foreigner. But not just any foreigner, a detested enemy. And she lived (along with her sister-in-law) with this enemy and his parents and brother. When the brothers and father died, only a family of women was left. Her mother-in-law, Naomi, told the girls to leave, to go back to their families, but Ruth refused.

"I will go with you," she protested. "I want to live where you live, and I want your God to be my God." Naomi accepted and the two women traveled back to Naomi's hometown. After the women's return, they eked out a living by gathering the grain left behind in the fields after the workers had harvested.

The biblical story of Ruth then veers into complicated legalities about transfer of property and women that makes the dramatic romantic like me a little impatient. Let's get to the good part! The part where Ruth goes to Naomi's cousin Boaz under cover of darkness, removes the blanket from his feet (and also, it is implied, some other bits, wink, wink) and spends the night with him although he cannot see her face. Let's get to the part were he realizes he's been tricked—and by whom. Let's get to the part about Boaz's unexpected generosity and kindness. Let's get to the part where in the due course of time, a baby is born to Ruth and Boaz, a baby who saves Naomi from a lifetime of grief and who, the story tells us, goes on to be Jesus' great-great-great-and-so-on-grandpa.

See, I used to think that this was a story of great romance, of drama.
The travel!

The illness and near starvation!

The baby that finally makes it all right!

I still love the story of Ruth. But now I see her story more simply, as a story of an ordinary life, a life lived kindly and with curiosity and love. Ruth follows her curiosity and her love into the fields. She follows her curiosity and her love into the tent of Boaz, where she uncovers his (wink, wink) feet. She's not a queen or a prophetess or Lady Gaga. She is a woman who survives, who keeps pedaling, up and down, up and down. A woman who follows the path where it leads and finally finds that it leads to the kind of adventure that comes from settling down. What Ruth's story offers, like what my real marriage to Jeff offers, is worth way more than all the drama I dreamed of as a girl.

If you think about it, her story is so ordinary that it's amazing Ruth's story got told at all, let alone remembered, let alone written down, let alone kept in this book so we could read it today, three thousand years later.

The story of Ruth says that in her time, the word of God was scarcely heard. Corruption, abuse, war, famine, oppression, mine-not-yours—those were the words on everyone's lips. Not Ruth, or as her name literally means, Kind Friendship. The word of God was scarce, but like a scrap, this one got saved, passed along, preserved. Kind Friendship.

I'm not named Ruth, after all. But I still hope I have a little bit of her in me. Ruth, who cares for people she has no business caring for. Ruth, who finds a way to make it in a world set up against her in every single way. Ruth, who in the end doesn't do anything all that extraordinary or famous or dramatic. Ruth, who keeps pedaling no matter what they shout at her out the windows of moving cars. Ruth. Kind Friendship.

THE BREATH JOURNALS: PART V

People are always telling me to breathe. A physician came to my church on Sunday morning to check me out and see if she wanted to hire me to officiate at an event.

At the end of the worship service, instead of smiling, shaking my hand, and saying hello as most people do, she poked me in the diaphragm.

"You need to breathe," she advised. (She also asked me to do the event, for what it's worth.)

Other people tell me this, too. Therapists. My husband. Good friends.

When my yoga teacher said the word "breathe," I took it personally until I realized he was talking to the whole class.

Sometimes someone in a meeting will glance over at me and then look around the room and say, "OK, now let's all take a nice deep breath." In those moments I think I must look like a person who doesn't breathe—parched, pinched, blue.

The more you think about it, the harder it is to do, it turns out. As I soon as I think, "I have to breathe!" then I start gasping.

Instead of telling me to breathe, from now on I would like it better if people would tell me to not think about breathing at all. So consider yourself notified. Next time you see me looking a little oxygen deprived, don't tell me to breathe, please.

Instead, tell me, "Stop thinking."

I'll know what you mean.

70

16 | *Parents, Feminism, and Being a Girl*

My favorite picture of my mom and dad together is a couple decades old now. In the picture, they are sitting at the end of our dining room table, laughing together over a plate of pasta. The table had been lavishly and lovingly set but now is in disarray. Some large group of people, probably a gang of my high school friends, have just stood up from it.

I like that picture, even though it marks the beginning of the end of their marriage. They did not sit together much after that.

My mom, actually, almost never sat still except when she was sunbathing. Even sunbathing, she radiated energy and tension. I would watch her while she lay on the deck chair, her body still but somehow quivering, drawing the sun to her, willing it to tan her. I believed she could do that.

I know three stories about my mom and what her life was like before I was born when she was nineteen years old.

The first is about mismatched shoes. She once wore one brown and one blue penny loafer to school. In the story as she told it, she told me she called her mom and cried. Her mother sold shoes at JC Penney and was something of a shoe expert.

"And she brought you another pair, right?" I prompted when she told me this story.

"Hmhmm."

She responded with uncharacteristic vagueness.

The second is this. When she was a small girl herself, she was looking after her younger brother when he ran in front of a car and was seriously injured. And my grandmother blamed her. "You were supposed to be watching him!" were the first words she yelled.

71

"But later, after he got better, she apologized, right, Mom?" I asked anxiously when she told me this story.

"Right," she nodded, eyes looking off at something I could not see.

Always connected in my mind to the story of the car accident is the third story. My mom was in the backseat of a car with her sister and brother on the way to get Easter pictures taken, and her sister threw up on their Easter finery. For some reason, I always imagined the car accident and the puke happening on the same day.

We weren't close to our extended family on either side, so I could never either corroborate or add to these mysterious snippets. Who were her neighbors? What were her friends' names? What books did she read or what little games of childhood did she play (besides rearranging the furniture in her room, which she claimed to do every weekend, a hobby I inherited from her)? She casually mentioned one time that she and her stepdad used to eat ice cream with potato chips crumpled on top. In my own childhood, we were rarely allowed even one of these forbidden fruits, let alone both together. If her childhood gave her any kindness, she never spoke of it except when she spoke of her maternal grandmother, whose exuberant sense of hospitality she inherited.

My mom was the kind of 1970s vegetarian peace activist who carried a subscription to *Ms* magazine before anyone else we knew used the word. Mom was a feminist who changed the words to the old hymns we sang on Sunday mornings to reflect a more inclusive sensibility. She took us kids to Take Back the Night marches in our strollers. On the other hand, in our house there was a pretty strict division of labor.

Once we were cleaning up the kitchen and I started to bag up the big juicy block from the garbage compactor.

"Oh, we don't take out the garbage."

She waved me away.

"That's why we have boys."

Evidently, we also had boys to mow the lawn, pump gas, carry heavy stuff, and pull our sleds back up hills. Naturally, I just figured I would marry the kind of boy who would do all those things and more. When

Jeff and I were first married, it was a bit of a shock to realize that he would never be that kind of boy.

Well, the years have passed and these days I don't bemoan anymore that Jeff can't pump the gas (and anyway, we moved to Oregon where it's the law that someone else has to do that). Now I relish doing the things that I used to think only boys did.

Picture me, for example, standing calf deep in a fast-moving stream. Elijah and I are splashing around and I see him plunge into the deep middle, his little arms pulling and this legs kicking. I splash in after him, shrieking with cold, surrendering to the pull of the water. Then we are out in the middle together.

As I float out, I look back up at the big rocks on the stream's edge. Other moms are lined up there, waving cameras and shouting encouragement to the kids and (looking around, I realize) other dads in the water. Jeff can't even make it to the riverbank, let alone the water. The roots and steps in the path make it impossible for him to get this far. He's high above us somewhere with his camera, contentedly taking pictures of trees on the smooth path overheard.

The rush of the water is thrilling. I think, not for the first or last time, "If I had an able bodied husband, I would never be here."

I would be on the rock, with the other moms. I would be observing, not doing. I would be sitting, not pushing against the current, feeling the delicious cold water on my skin and the shifting pebbles underfoot.

I would be on the side of the road, waiting for the cyclists to pass, not pedaling a bike of my own.

Jeff used to tell me that he did not want his disability to be limiting for Elijah and me. At the beginning, I used to hang back with him instead of trying new things. Later, with Jeff's encouragement, I tried to experience new things on his behalf, but I did it reluctantly because I knew he could not and I felt that someone should. Now, I plunge in, because I want to.

It is not easy for Jeff to be sidelined as often as he is. But the two-sided coin of our life together is the unexpected sweetness of the opportunities that his disability sometimes provides to me.

If he were able to jump in the water with the other dads, he no doubt would. He would be the one to catch our son in strong arms, to laugh and lift the dripping child overhead. I know he feels the loss of these little moments, and so do I. But in the weird way that one of life's realities can be both gift and curse, his loss has become a gain for both of us.

I am the one in the river. If Jeff were able-bodied, I would be sitting on the rock now. I would not dive in. I would sit and watch. "Oh," I would think, "I don't do that. That's why we have boys."

Having an active young son has helped push me to my limits, too. I guess it's no accident that I'm running my first sprint triathlon on the tenth birthday of our only son. Before running the sprint triathlon, the most athletic thing I've ever done was give birth.

When I was pregnant, the one thing Jeff and I wanted to spare the child was time in the hospital. Jeff has muscular dystrophy; I had a tricky heart that required surgery. We remembered back to all our childhood days in and out of hospitals. We prayed that we could give our child different memories than those. Ten years to the day before the day I ran the tri, I woke from a dream of being in labor to realize that I was, in fact, in labor. But that was impossible because it was a month early. Our hopes for Elijah did not save him from ten days in the NICU.

The morning I went into labor, my mom got on a plane immediately. By the time it got dark, we were looking together over the edge of the incubator. Kind people in our wonderful little church washed my feet at the baby shower they'd planned to take place before the birth but that we held anyway. Those wonderful church friends stayed away when we asked them to, held the baby when we were ready to hand him over, prayed, and brought us so much more food than we could eat. My soul sister JJ, eight-and-three-quarters-months pregnant herself, came to the hospital with her husband, Steve, after I had been sitting in the NICU for days and days. JJ and Steve held my hands and coaxed, "Come outside, the sun is shining."

I thought I couldn't leave the baby even for a minute, but I did. We did not walk far down the sunny bike path outside the hospital, crowded with winter-soaked women and men and children drying out in the first spring rays of sun, but it was enough. Enough to warm up as much from their kindness as from the sunny day.

JJ and her husband and their kids, our God-family, keep holding their hands out to us. They continue to walk us out into the light. We share a meal most every Sunday night. Imagine such an evening. Kids are playing a game of make believe involving a jump rope, a wooden sword, and someone's Scooby Doo costume from last Halloween. JJ is telling me about a book she's reading, I'm peeling veggies and Steve is putting plates on the table. Jeff asks if anyone wants to listen to music.

This is not lifting or transferring Jeff; it is not getting him dressed or helping him shower. But Sunday night dinner, with its ease and familiarity, its distinct lack of company manners and the smell of good food, helps me carry him nonetheless.

One Sunday night, over pot roast, baked potatoes, and some kind of vegetables, my six-year-old godson smiled shyly and announced that he had a loose tooth, his first. Then he told a story about his friend who'd had a loose tooth not long ago. As his dad tucked the friend into bed, he had joked, "I'll just go get my rusty pliers and pull that thing out."

The friend did not wait—during the night he took a pair of toy plastic pliers and pulled the tooth out himself.

"And then he was sad because the Tooth Fairy did not come. But I know the Tooth Fairy is not real, I know it's . . ." and he stuck out his thumb, like he was trying to hitch a ride from JJ, next to him ". . . my mom and dad."

Elijah, grinning from the other side of the table, teased, "Should I go get the string? We could tie that tooth to a doorknob."

"No wayyyy!"

And everyone laughed, even the loose-tooth boy.

I don't remember believing in the Tooth Fairy either. I don't remember getting a quarter or a nickel or whatever teeth were going for those days under my pillow. I've always thought this was good because I don't remember having that traumatic "learning there is no Tooth Fairy" (or Santa, for that matter) moment. But I do remember the string and the doorknob.

When I was about six, one of my teeth was loose—the big one in front on the right. I kept pushing it with my tongue, and wiggling with my finger, feeling the sharp edges on the top of the tooth. But it would not come out. It seemed to be hanging by one little piece of gum that just would not break. I don't know where my mom got the string and doorknob idea.

"See, I'll just tie this piece of string around your tooth, tie the other end around the doorknob, slam the door and then the tooth will pop right out."

She got the string tied around the knob, a fancy old brass one, worn smooth except for the flowers and swirls etched around the edges. She got the string tied around my tooth and pulled the tiny wet knot tight.

Then I opened my mouth and screamed and screamed and screamed. As it turned out, my mom did not have the heart to slam the door. Instead she wiggled the little tooth noose off as carefully as she could while I kept screaming. I was scared in the moment, but every time I think of it now, I laugh, and I think of my mom, who tried to spare me the momentary shock and pain of a tooth pulled but gave herself the much bigger pain of trying to get that slippery little piece of string off my fragile, wiggly little tooth.

We don't always get it right, these little families we make. Sometimes, trying to ease one another's pain, we just make more of a mess. But more often than not, we rest in one another. In those times, I can coast and feel the delicious wind in my hair and remember that I don't ride alone. In those times, I pray that everyone can, one day, know they ride with someone too.

17 | *In the Family Photo Album of Good and Evil*

It's not just the God-family we have made that coasts along beside us. Our families, wherever they come from, give us story after story to carry. Some stories are heavy, some light. Here's one.

My great-uncle John tried to kill his wife, but she lived.

Wait. Let me back up. My great-uncle John (who, as son of Alleluia and brother of Maranatha, really lucked out in the name department, if you ask me) was, like his brother and father, a missionary in India. If you go to southern India today and stick your head in a Christian church, you might find some very old person there who remembers him with fondness. Remembers his tireless energy, his concern for people, and his fervent desire to help souls know and love Christ as he did.

His family remembers that, too. And remembers this. Walking along a mountain path with his wife, arguing about his extramarital affair with another missionary, he pushed her in a rage off that narrow path and down the mountainside. I've had a chance to be in India and on that path on that mountain. It's so steep and rocky that, even sitting, you have to brace your feet firmly, use your stomach muscles to keep from falling. It wouldn't have taken much for someone to lose her balance, especially if that someone was in the impractical shoes and long hot dresses Western women insisted on wearing in those days, even in tropical climates. It would not have taken much of a shove to send her down the mountain.

I try to imagine what happened then. Seeing what he had done, was John immediately struck with horror? Did he slide down after her, to arrive at the bottom almost as soon as she did? Or did he pause, look down, wonder if she was finally gone? And then, later, how did he get her out?

There was no one for miles in any direction in this deserted place. He must have carried her himself, I guess.

She did not die, the wife of great-uncle John whose name I can never remember. She lived, for years and years, in terrible pain and agony from the many breaks and bruises she sustained in that fall. They stayed married. But John says that, as she died at last, she whispered words of forgiveness there on her deathbed. Could she have, really? It depends on the mood I'm in, whether I can believe that or not.

My great-grandfather, John's father, Alleluia Irenaeus, was a missionary in India, too. There is a family story that one time he talked his way into Gandhi's home (yes, the Gandhi) when that holy man was on some kind of retreat and not officially receiving visitors. My great-grandfather told Gandhi that he must accept Jesus as his Lord and Savior if he did not want to go to hell.

Gandhi replied, "What Christ is for your people, I am for my people."

This angered by great-grandfather, who left the house. Gandhi died a few months later, slain by an assassin's bullet. It was one of the great sorrows and regrets of my great-grandfather's life that Gandhi cried, "Hey, Ram!" instead of calling on the name of Christ in his last moments.

I have to admire Alleluia's, well, . . . whatever the fundamentalist Christian version of chutzpa is. In many ways I have probably followed in his footsteps. But I emphatically cannot believe in a God who consigns a man like Gandhi to hell because he did not say the magic word at the right time.

I was working in a grocery store and trying to decide whether to go to seminary or not, talking about my great-grandfather while a co-worker and I stacked boxes of cereal on the shelves. He knew I was thinking about going to seminary, but I was trying to talk myself out of it.

"I don't think I can really be a pastor," I said. "Christianity is responsible for so much that is despicable! Wars and intolerance and, and, and . . . Christian rock."

My friend looked at me with wise, sad eyes.

"Oh, Jennifer, you don't really think that the history books tell the whole story, do you? They tell one side. But for every despicable act, there is a loving one. We hear all the time about the terrible acts, but the loving ones are often hidden. Speak for the loving acts instead."

What I have learned is that the two are sometimes so closely intertwined that it is hard to tell them apart. My great-grandfather, earnestly burdened by the weight of Gandhi's lost soul, burst in on the holy man. Loving? Despicable? Or an equal measure of both?

I used to believe that most people were mostly one thing or another. But, riding a bike, I have come to realize that what keeps us up and moving forward is not leaning too heavily to one side or another. Riding a bike, I have come to see that balance comes because we rely first on one leg, and then the other—over, up, and around. I wonder if it's the same with our personalities? If so, I want to understand these despicable, loving people. After all, whatever else they are, they are my family, my heritage. They are not just riding along. Someone carries—I carry—their stories deep inside.

So I go looking for other stories of other missionaries. I read, trying to find clues into who they were and, more than that, why they were. I learn that the complicated legacy of missionaries cannot be understood in isolation. For instance, in the 1880s, the Hawaiian government began sending people diagnosed (or misdiagnosed) with leprosy to the tiny, isolated peninsula of Kalaupapa on the tiny, isolated island of Molokai. What the government intended was for the first boatload or two of patients to die, thus ridding the islands of leprosy forever. What happened instead was an unintentionally long-term public health policy that lasted nearly a hundred years.

There are many diseases that are more contagious than leprosy. But the Board of Health did not send people with mumps or small pox into exile—only people with leprosy. A mistranslation of the word for any skin disorder or rash in the Old Testament of the Bible probably lies at the root of this decision. Thanks to three thousand years of religious tradition, "leper" (an extremely offensive word to people with leprosy, by the way, and one I do not use lightly) means not just a person with an illness but one who should be shunned. But it was religious tradition that also brought doctors, house builders, and gravediggers (often in the same person) to the island. It was religious tradition that gave the exiles a sense of community, of purpose, and of hope. So what story do we tell? The despicable one or the loving one?

Maybe all we can do is hold them up side by side and say, "All of this is what it means to be a human being."

There are still people on Kalaupapa today who were diagnosed with leprosy in the 1940s and '50s, although the entire facility is now a national park. Without an invitation from a resident, the only way to visit Kalaupapa is to contract with a tour group, which I did when I went to Hawaii in 2013.

One of the first things we were told in no uncertain terms was that we were not to try to make contact with the patients in Kalaupapa. So many photos have been taken exploiting them, so many stories have been told about their so-called pathetic state, and they have been sensationalized too much.

But by chance, I got to meet one of the patients, and we talked for a few minutes in the dust by the side the volleyball court, where he was drawing lines for that night's game.

As we stood on the sidelines of the volleyball court, the patient told me a story that I'd read somewhere before about thinking that everyone he saw was a cowboy when he'd been exiled to Kalaupapa at fourteen. Later he learned that the handkerchiefs he saw the other patients wearing around their necks were covers for tracheotomy tubes.

"It must have been hard to leave your family at such a young age."

"Oh yes, it was the hardest thing I ever had to do." It seemed like there might have been tears for a moment but then the moment passed. The patient told me that his father had asked him to come back to Honolulu when the ban on people with leprosy was lifted. He replied, "No."

"Here I can ride horses, go fishing. It's the perfect life for a boy."

The impression I got from him was not of exploitation or grief or even powerful resiliency—although there were all of those in his story. The real impression I had was of a man just living his life as best as he could. He was just pedaling up and down, up and down. And now and then he could coast and feel the wind in his face.

I don't know why this surprised me. After all, this is what Jeff and I want, too. For you not to feel sorry for us, to imagine our life is much harder than yours, but to recognize that we are more like you than it may seem at first.

It seems absurd that I had to go all the way from Oregon to Hawaii to realize this. I guess you don't have to fly across an ocean to recognize how alike we all are. You can get it from your cat-lady neighbor, or the heavily mascaraed clerk at the grocery store, or even from the roommate who never changes the toilet paper roll. But I know that it works to get connected by getting totally away, because it's happened to me before.

Long ago, I got the chance to travel with my dad to India, to visit some of the places where he had grown up as a missionary kid. Coming home on the plane from Mumbai to Amsterdam, I sat near an adoption agency employee who was taking two baby girls to the Netherlands. Since regulations only allowed him to hold one baby, he asked me to hold the other one during the flight. All day the baby had been passed from stranger to stranger. When the stewardess handed her to me, she began to wail with a piercing, tired little cry.

Her arms and legs were thin and her hair smelled sweaty. I held her, rocked her as well as I could in the cramped seat, sang quietly in her perfect little ear. I told her not to worry, that she was going to people who loved her. As I said it, I prayed that it was true and I cried a little, too, for all she had lost. She wailed for perhaps half an hour, and I kept holding her and talking, and after a while she stopped crying. But she didn't sleep. Her eyes were wide awake.

In her book *Daring Greatly*, Brene Brown says that our own vulnerability terrifies us, while we are drawn to other people's vulnerability like moths to flame. "We love seeing raw truth and openness in other people, but we're afraid to let them see it in us."[7]

When people turn to check out Jeff in his wheelchair, or I hold a baby on a plane and weep, or you marvel at the inspiring stories of people with leprosy in Kalaupapa, what we respond to is vulnerability. We like it when the vulnerability is obvious because we think we know what we can respond to.

The thing is, though, that everyone has a story, an obstacle to overcome, an area of vulnerability. The real obstacle may or may not be the one you can see. Of the orphan or the dude in a wheelchair or the guy with leprosy or even Gandhi the holy man himself, ask what you would ask of anyone, "When you worry at night, what do you worry about?" and "What makes you feel most alive?" or even "What do you like about volleyball?"

THE BREATH JOURNALS: PART VI

Breathe.
Flow, gurgle, hum, purr,
ripple, rumble,
susurrate, insufflate,
inhale, exhale,
gasp, gulp, pant, puff,
expire, respire,
sniff, snort, sigh,

---

7. Brene Brown, *Daring Greatly: How the Courage to Be Vulnerable Transforms the Way We Live, Love, Parent, and Lead* (New York: Gotham/Penguin Group, 2012), 41.

wheeze, murmur,
eupnoea.

Wait. Eupnoea?

The dictionary says "eupnoea" is "easy, free respiration, as is observed nor-
mally under resting conditions" and also says "During eupnoea, neural output
to respiratory muscles is highly regular, with rhythmic bursts of activity dur-
ing inspiration only to the diaphragm and external intercostal muscles."

Eupnoea. I want to name something eupnoea, but I can't decide if it should
be a creamy dessert or a pet cat or a slow, sexy dance.

Or maybe a poem, a found one, like this.

During eupnoea,
output to muscles
is
highly regular,
with rhythmic bursts
of activity
during inspiration.

18 | *Puke on the Plane*

Sometimes plane rides bring you toward strangers so you can know them
better. Other times, they bring you right into yourself or face to face
with someone you love. It was like that this one time we flew back home
to Oregon from visiting family in Minnesota. It had been a trying ten-
day visit during which none of us slept, I cried a lot, and Jeff and I had

our least favorite fight ever. But we had made it. It was over. Until two hours into the flight, when Eli woke from a sound sleep, puking. Not one of those polite little delicate pukes either. Actually, if there are polite, delicate little pukes, I've never really experienced one, either as a participant or a bystander.

I must have taken off my headphones somehow, but I don't really remember that part. I do remember yanking all those slippery magazines and odd-size pamphlets out of the cloth pocket in front of me, trying to find the bag they are supposed to keep there. Also, trying to gently murmur at eight-year-old Eli while wrestling him with all my strength to keep him from obeying his half-awake, wholly horrified fight or flight instinct. With some third arm I grew just for the occasion, I also somehow pressed the button for the flight attendant.

I couldn't believe how calm I was, except for being unreasonably put out to be interrupted three-quarters of the way through the in-flight movie. It was this edgy family drama with Paul Giamatti as a dysfunctional wrestling coach. "Now it's probably in the purgatory between theater release and DVD, and it'll be months before I know how it ends." I actually had this thought.

Except for that, I felt totally present, like a Zen Buddhist three days into one of those meditation retreats where they help you explore the spiritual depths of mindfully washing the dishes. I glanced at the wall of the bulkhead and thought, mildly, considering, "That is a lot of vomit."

The first flight attendant arrived with one of those flimsy plastic glasses, half full of ginger ale. Given the cataclysmic and still unfolding state of events, ginger ale was really the very last thing we needed.

A bag. Please, a bag. Because he was still throwing up. I kept monologuing meaningless encouragement, "Wow, what a bummer, dude. That feels rotten, huh? OK, you're doing great."

Absent the bag, we made a sort of sack and also a towel out of my husband's vest. Somehow, I managed to reach into the vest's left-hand pocket for an old phone Jeff let Elijah play video games on. I forgot my hearing aids in the right-hand pocket, though.

A taller and smarter flight attendant arrived, wearing blue gloves and carrying, finally, a bag. This one was not the lunch-sized wax-paper sack I was expecting, but instead it was gigantic, red, with a hazardous waste symbol on the outside.

We filled it.

By the end, we had added to the bag the following, which I inventoried in my head as if I might file some alternate universe insurance claim, although as far as I know our travel insurance carried no puke rider. Elijah's slippers (for days afterward when someone asked him about the trip, he'd say sadly, "I lost my slippers on the airplane"), the cheap black sweatshirt he became a ninja in, an absurdly expensive water bottle I'd gotten at REI, the vest my husband wore every day, all those slippery magazines. And, did I mention, my hearing aids?

The clothes we were wearing, we had to keep or go naked, although both Eli and I looked and smelled like . . . Well, there's no metaphor that's apt here, except to say that we were exactly like people who'd been puked on in an airplane. Someone brought more towels, and, unexpectedly, coffee grounds to sprinkle on the mess, which seemed to include us, too, because quite a lot of the black specks ended up on our clothes and sticky summer skin.

The captain announced that we were beginning our descent. We left our seats in direct violation of the illuminated seat-belt sign and marched through to the first-class bathroom which, just like the one in back, has a ridiculous sink, an ineffectual trickle of water. I was expecting something grander. Somehow, Elijah and I both took off our clothes, rinsed them in the tiny sink, put them back on wet.

Jeff, of course, couldn't help with any of the physical part of this, but I leaned on him anyway. I counted on him to dispatch the stupid flight attendant and summon the smarter one, took comfort from his soft rumble in my ear. The big, important argument we'd had at my mom's cabin the night before was the furthest thing from our minds. I couldn't really hear him (I did mention the hearing aids, right?) although he was probably murmuring lovingly: "Oh my God, what did he *eat?*" Trying to work out how this could have happened is his default line-of-thought in the face of illness.

Later, we'll joke we should have paid attention to the dire portents and not boarded the plane. Actually, we are only half joking. The problem is, once you choose to follow signs, which ones do you pick? That original, undefined Bad Feeling we both had before we bought the ticket to visit our families in the first place; or the later one, after the tickets were already riding heavily on our credit card?

Anyway, maybe it was not the whole vacation we were being warned against, just the return plane ride. We got to the airport hours early, like we always do, and the plane was already late arriving from Atlanta. They kept saying this at the gate, emphasizing the "AtLANta," as if the city itself was responsible for the delay.

This delay might not have been a bad omen, actually, but a good one because it gave us time for an unexpected stop in the family bathroom in the airport. Boy, bags, woman, man, wheelchair were all crowded into the hot little bathroom while I helped Jeff get on the toilet and then off again.

Or maybe, we will joke again, we should have been forewarned against getting on the plane by the claxon in the airport, which started while we were in the bathroom, somewhere between helping Jeff get cleaned up and transferring him back to the wheelchair. There was a little snag with the transfer. The medical supply belt we usually use for this lift had been checked since we didn't plan on this detour. But we were able to figure out the right combination of physics, torque, and brute force required for the lift from wheelchair to toilet and toilet back to wheelchair while the alarm went on and on.

The alarm was definitely a portent, we will agree later, as was the warning voice over the loudspeaker that continued for more than an hour. "A fire has been detected in the airport. Please follow directions of fire safety personnel." Impatient to obey the rules, as always, Eli mildly panicked. Jeff cracked a joke and said something reassuring. It really was very hot in that bathroom. I wiped Jeff and soothed Elijah and sweated.

Finally we were done and out into the wide, cool, smokeless hallway, where the alarm was still sounding. We returned to the gate and the placid faces of our fellow passengers, who were still reading, napping, and talking on cell phones as if warnings were not being loudly broadcast right in our ears.

We got on the plane, and all seemed well but that was so three hours ago, before the epic puke. Now the flight was really almost over because Look! Lights! And then it was over, and Eli and I ran up the jetway, shivering and blinking in the fluorescents, damp as newborns, grinning with relief.

If you saw us, you might have shaken your head. You might have thought how desolate this all looks—the wheelchair, the hearing aids (lost, alas!), and now, like frosting on some bitter cake, all this throw-up.

Once, I would have thought so, too. But now I know it's just life. During the whole long, ridiculous day I'd had access to that astonishing peace that comes from knowing just what to do and doing it without complaint or hesitation. Lift, love, laugh, comfort, clean up, keep calm. The wheels had kept going around and around. I had that perfect sense of peace that comes from doing exactly what you are supposed to be doing, and doing it with ease.

It was 2:37 A.M., our time. If you saw us that early, early morning, this is what you would have seen. A woman with circles under her eyes and vomit on her sandals, holding her son's hand next to baggage claim, reading lips and nodding agreement to words she could not hear, waiting for a man in a wheelchair to be carried off an airplane. If you had seen us, you would have seen all those bedraggled people smiling. We were not, as you might have supposed, pedaling all that hard. We were coasting, almost home.

19 | *Seeing the Light from the Yoga Mat*

The sensation of coming home and being home was so unfamiliar for so long. For most of my life, I had a restless certainty that I belonged somewhere other than where I was. I got glimpses of feeling at home, but they were few and far between.

I first studied yoga a long time ago, when a professor's yoga instructor named Vijay visited a seminary class. We pushed the desks out of the way and lay on the industrial carpeting and practiced breathing. One person refused to participate because she had heard that yoga was not Christian (News flash! It is not!). I was pretty sure that although nothing Christian was happening, nothing evil was happening either. In fact, it was both comforting and invigorating, which, in my way of thinking, is what Jesus is all about. I wanted more. I found out that Vijay had a studio in his home not far from where I was living, so I dropped in on a class.

I had no idea what I was doing, and really I was then, as I continue to be to this day, a deeply mediocre student of yoga. I shared the classes with my friend Rachel who is more physically flexible than me, and who took to it with a lot more grace. But if you studied with Vijay, it sort of didn't matter if you were really good at yoga or not.

I just found out that Vijay died last year, the day before Thanksgiving. He was not too old, but his kidneys, they said, just gave out. Which seems impossible. Because Vijay's yard, his house, his yoga class seem like they are eternally there, ready and waiting, every Thursday morning just the same. It feels like I should be able to give you these directions, even now. It feels like I should be able to tell you that if you are ever in Seattle some Thursday morning, this is what you should do.

To get to Vijay's house, you walk to the end of a tree-lined street and open a tall gate. His yard is not huge, but part of the magic of the place is that you feel that you've entered a new little country. You walk down a winding path and cross the tiny creek. Notice the flowers and the birds. There are lots of them to notice. On your journey through the yard you may want to rest on one of the benches. Take your time.

The studio is a daylight basement with shelves of books, a fire going in the fireplace, and (instead of plastic mats) comfy wool blankets. Put a five-dollar bill in the overflowing bowl of money. If you get there half an hour early, you will be in time for the teaching, which is a reading from an ancient Indian book followed by a conversation, usually about how you should love everyone.

During the class, you will learn a lot about sun salutation, which Vijay reveres. You will sometimes do only variations on sun salutations for more than an hour. Your teacher will occasionally make little sounds of delight, as if he's eating something delicious. "Mmmmm, now *that* feels very good to the body," he will exclaim. This will make you giggle, but he is right, it does feel good to the body.

Savasana at Vijay's studio is done exactly how I always thought Jesus would do it. After you lie on your back, in the pose of a corpse, Vijay will gently lay a soft kleenex and then an eye pillow on your eyes. He will ask you if you'd like to be covered with a blanket or two, if you'd like a pillow under your knees. He will do this for everyone—the eight or so ladies (one of them is older than eighty, I think)—who lie in a row in the sun coming in through the windows. Then he will walk from person to person, placing woodstove-warmed stones in the palms of your hands. The rest you will experience for the next ten minutes will be as rejuvenating as a full night of sleep.

Sometimes during those ten minutes you will actually sleep. You may fall into REM sleep and have something like a dream. One time I had a vision, one that I bring back even now to raise my spirits.

After savasana, you may be reluctant to rise, but when you do, you will sit around the woodstove with the ladies. While Vijay gives you tea he has made, someone will get out a tin of cookies she has baked. People will gossip gently or talk about travels or gardening or children. They will dote on you if you are younger than they are, and you will almost certainly be younger than they are. Vijay is no spring chicken himself—he once won a weight lifting competition in the 65-and-up division—and he draws an older crowd.

It was during one of the post-yoga tea times that I heard the following interchange:

"She can't come to yoga anymore; she had a baby."

"Oh really? I didn't know she was married . . ."

"Well, she went swimming with this guy at Coleman Pool."

At the time, I thought that was hilarious, an echo of the urban legend that if you went swimming with a guy it could make you pregnant. And also, more seriously and righteously, I thought that nothing would keep me from Vijay's class.

But then I did get pregnant (not from swimming—from the usual way) and all that downward facing dog just really was no good for the nausea. And if you're thinking that what with all the teaching, the yoga itself, the deep rest, and the cookies, it must have been a long class, you are right. The whole thing took the better part of the morning, and with a coughy little baby to look after, who has time for that? And a five-dollar yoga class is a real good deal until you're paying someone thirty-five dollars to babysit for the morning, and then it's harder to justify. And then there was work and then we moved across town and I couldn't walk to the magical little studio anymore.

I gave up yoga then, but the vision I had that day stayed. It was like a vision of being home. I saw myself lying in a warm and comfortable room, surrounded by loving friends. I saw my inner self, my soul, as I usually perceived her. She was a cloudy and somehow also gooey human shape. She was writhing in self-pity and an anxious sense that nothing was right in the world, herself most of all. Then I saw her as the loving friends saw her, as Jesus saw her. She was not cloudy or gooey. She did not writhe. She was balanced, good and bad, and her soul shone with a pure, pure light. That light shone into the warm room, across the dozing ladies, out into all the world.

20 | *How'd I Move Out of This Body Anyway?*

I don't always remember that I am light, of course. I forget and then I remember. I forget and then I remember again. I lose my balance, tip over, get up again a little scraped, but ready to try again. I know I will never again lie on the floor in Vijay's warm, soft room. But I can remember what that's like, remember what it's like to be light.

And I try to help other people remember the light, when I can. Pretty much every summer my dear friend JJ and I lead a women's retreat called Women of the 14th Moon. It is a ceremony invented in modern times by three women who wanted to address women's fear of aging. It's a new thing to do, but like some ancient rite, it is passed word of mouth, woman to woman. Our ritual is short, lasting the better part of a morning, but I know of ceremonies that last a whole weekend, three days of singing, celebrating, dancing around a fire. Each year, as we honor and celebrate three stages of womanhood, we honor the youngest women among us by telling stories about our first menses. These are stories of pain, confusion, unexpected compassion. There is a lot of laughter as we share what we thought we knew and what we had yet to learn.

I usually tell the part where I had borrowed my mom's white nightgown and was having trouble sleeping because I had a terrible stomachache. My mom's nightgown was cotton, with ruffles around the neck.

It was long and flowy and tangled around my legs. I rolled up with stomach cramps, and then I had blood on my mom's nightgown.

I remember going to find my mom. I remember her telling me what was happening with a face that was twisted like she could have cried, if my mom was a crier, which she wasn't.

But I don't tell the next part, the part about being at camp, the part when I really realized what it would mean to be a woman in the world. Girls were a mystery to me. I was used to hanging out with boys. With boys, there were certain things to prove, but not the same things, and I knew how to work around them by pretending to be too superior for their games of chance and brawn. Girls, with their changing alliances and small cruelties, were a total mystery to me.

I was a real country kid in those days. I was at this all-girl camp for three weeks and so countrified that I was totally awed by the cool urbanity of the big-city girls from Oshkosh, Wisconsin, who made up most of my cabin-mates. I wish I could remember their names, but I can't. I can remember one of them, talking to another in the common shower, but loudly enough for me to hear.

"I mean, I don't care if you shave your legs, but if you don't shave your armpits, that's just disgusting."

Was shaving something I was supposed to do now?

I remember another of them, in the middle of the cabin, one hip thrust out, hairbrush in hand.

"Ew. Gross. Who's leaving these pads in the garbage?"

Everyone looked at me, well known as the only person in the cabin to be menstruating. My face burned and I whispered, "Not me."

Where was I supposed to put the used pads? I actually did not know. But I figured out then that unwrapped and in the common room trash basket was probably wrong.

As far as I remember, I attended that camp on a full scholarship for three years, a total of nine weeks, and did not make a single friend. I took refuge so often in the library, a little-used but comfy tiny little nest up a flight of stairs on the outside of the dining hall, that Grownups talked to me about it, told me they would be keeping track to make sure that I was Spending Time with Others.

We were supposed to learn swimming, boating, horseback riding, and shooting, so I did. I learned how to stay afloat for a minute in all my clothes—barely. I learned how to wait in the middle of the lake for a lifeguard to come and rescue me and my swamped sunfish boat. I learned that if I did not kick the horse, he would not run. I learned that I liked shooting a gun more than I thought I would—and that I was better at it than I would imagine.

But mostly I learned two things. The first thing I learned was to avoid other girls in groups. At the closing campfire, we'd scream as the music director told us a story about the camp monster, who had once been an ordinary man until he stepped on the end of a rake and the blow to his head made him stronger than a regular human, and also immortal. We would be so terrified that we would shriek and grab the girl next to us no matter how we had felt about each other until then. And we would walk back to the cabin through the dark woods, yelling and clutching each other for dear life. It was the only moment in the whole three weeks I felt included.

The second thing I learned was that my body was too much. Not only was I too hairy and razorless. I was also way too tall, a head taller at least than all the Oshkosh cutie pies. Without deodorant, which evidently I was supposed to be applying, I smelled bad. And I was far too prone to excretions that apparently I did not know how to handle.

I carried that awkward girl with me into adulthood. Until Jeff, who did not seem to find me too squishy or ishy. Who does not just tolerate my body's curves and jiggles, but unabashedly claims to lust for them. I tower over Jeff as he sits in his wheelchair, but being with him I do not feel, for once, too tall or hairy or smelly or wrong.

I love his body, too. Jeff's body, don't get me wrong, is weird. He has no muscle tone at all in his long, skinny arms and legs. His tummy is round and so are the bottoms of his soft feet. But from our first night of intimacy, our bodies have just worked together, my curves nestling into his curves as if, almost as if, our curves were made for each other.

THE BREATH JOURNALS: PART VII

After I badgered him awhile about his snoring, Jeff went in for a sleep study. The techs led him into a perfectly dark and soundless room, put sticky pads attached to wires all over his body, trained a camera on him, and told him to go to sleep. Somehow, he did. Sort of.

When the techs woke him up in the morning, they told him it looked on camera like he was sleeping. He was not just snoring, though. According to the wires, he was actually choking and stopping breathing, fifty to sixty times every single hour.

Now he breathes through a mask a night, a CPAP. Asking around, it turns out more people than I'd think breathe at night this way. The machine is not quiet, and at first it was hard to sleep with it in the room. Now, I listen for it. The rise and fall and wheeze of the machine sounds as natural as breath now.

21 | *A Caregiver's Complicated Dance*

During the tri training, I was falling asleep just fine. After all, I was exercising more than I ever had before. But forty-five minutes later, I would be wide awake, thrashing and twitching. What could be keeping me awake? Was I worried? I didn't feel particularly worried. But then I worried that I was worried and didn't know it.

94

After a couple of weeks, it occurred to me that the reason I was waking up from a sound sleep was because my legs were cramping. It was so like me not to have any idea what my body was doing and thinking it was all some kind of problem of my mind, some stress I had not addressed, some hidden anxiety. The leg cramps were pretty easily solved with stretches before bed, but I added leg cramps to the long list of extra time-killers the sprint triathlon training was adding to my already impossibly packed schedule. I started to fantasize about quitting the training, started to imagine everything else I could do if I did not have spend three minutes stretching my legs before bed each night.

Honestly, it was like being in my body was a full-time job.

One night when I stretched my legs, I glanced at Jeff bundled under a pile of blankets (Jeff is always cold) and I remembered the first time I had ever seen him lying in bed. We weren't even lovers then. It was back in the tender, tentative early days of our friendship. Jeff called me at home (it was so long ago, we didn't even have cell phones then) as I was on the way out the door to the office where we both worked. He was stuck in bed and he needed help getting up and would I come over? He asked this fast and low, embarrassed.

At his apartment, he talked me through helping him up without meeting my eye. I got him settled in the bathroom, started to help him change the sheets, which had gotten soiled, but he pled with me to leave them. A couple hours later, at the office, he handed me a flower.

"I want to thank you again, so much, for what you did for me this morning."

"Really, it was no big deal." Now I was the embarrassed one, flushing and unable to meet his intent gaze.

"It was to me."

That was not the last time I would help Jeff with something he physically was not able to do. Not by a long shot. Incidentally, it was not the last time he gave me flowers either. I had not read Brene Brown's writing about the power of vulnerability, but it is no exaggeration to say I fell totally in love with Jeff the day he called me first when he was stuck.

I am Jeff's wife before I am anything else to anyone else—before I am a pastor or a daughter or a friend or even a mother. But I am something else too. Besides his wife, I am also his caregiver.

When there is a disabled person in the family, the role of the caregiver depends on many things. What the caregiver must do depends on the financial, spiritual, and psychological resources of the caregiver. It depends on the severity of the disability, the danger the disabled person poses to him- or herself and others, the other responsibilities of both the caregiver and the disabled person. It depends on the time available to both the caregiver and the disabled person, the space and how effectively it is set up, other persons—paid and not—who are available to help with the caregiving, the equipment available and how suited the equipment is the particular disability.

Caregiving is a complicated dance of intimacy, resentment, mental resiliency, and physical exertion. As much as I wish sometimes that Jeff were not disabled at all, as much as I slip sometimes into daydreams of him being strong, I cherish the closeness that caregiving has brought to us. Whatever distance creeps into our married life, at the end of the day, there is always a familiar and, in its way, comforting touch. I wrap my arms around his torso for a transfer and slide my hands under his knees for a lift. He places one light hand on my shoulder to steady himself. We are connected physically, even if we are both quiet and lost in our own thoughts.

I bend my head to remove his shoes, and he whispers an old joke in my ear and we both shake with laughter. He sighs with contentment at the stretch of legs that have been bent with sitting all day. It's pleasurable for me too, smoothing the sheet under his resting body so that he is perfectly comfortable.

I cherish the knowledge I have of what his body needs for comfort. Cherish that this is knowledge only I have. Jeff does not lift me or help me dress, but he knows what I need for comfort, too. He knows how to soothe me to sleep with a brush of his hand on mine or with the sound of his slow, deep voice reading from a familiar book. He knows when to call my office, tell them I'm having a sick day, and send me to bed. He knows when a banana will cure what ails me, or a fast walk, or a *Doctor Who* marathon.

In a physical therapist's office, I helped him from his wheelchair to the exam table. We have done this lift hundreds of times, but every time it takes a level of concentration and communication I imagine trapeze artists use. So I was concentrating, my grip on the side of his jeans, our bodies close. I was surprised when the PT applauded once Jeff was safely on the bed.

"That was the best transfer I have ever seen! Really, you two are so sweet and patient with each other, it is a joy to watch."

All of these are pleasures. But, of course, it is not all pleasure. As often as we are sweet and patient with each other, we grinch and growl. Sometimes caregiving is just plain physically exhausting. Sometimes, one more lift seems like one more than tired limbs can perform. Other times, it is psychologically wearing. The legs straighten, but only to cramp and ache more, instead of less. The sheet will not smooth.

Sometimes I resent his need.

Sometimes he resents my freedom.

Sometimes nothing is going wrong, exactly. Sometimes we are both just cranky or distracted or would rather be somewhere else.

In our dance together, we do what we can to balance the connection and the distance, the intimacy and the resentment. One of our solutions is to ask for help. Several times a week, we pay helpers to assist Jeff in getting ready in the morning.

Like Jeff, his older brother Andy has SMA. Andy's wife, Laurie, is what they used to call a pistol. When Jeff and I had been dating a little while, and I met him at Andy and Laurie's house for the family Christmas party, I watched them both in amazement. Jeff's disability and wheelchair were still so new and exotic to me. Laurie and Andy, in their cozy house in the world's friendliest cul-de-sac and their two little blonde kids running around, seemed to have it all figured out. If they could navigate this life, I thought, we could too. I do not possess Laurie's indomitable, cheerful energy, though. In addition to working full time (more!) and volunteering for several organizations and raising two of the most delightful young people I have ever met, she is the sole caregiver for my brother-in-law. I used to think I would be just like that, but I have found I cannot do it alone. This was an unpleasant shock for me, and I think for Jeff too, but over time we negotiate what I can and am willing to do, and what needs help.

The future for Jeff will bring more caregiving, not less. There will be more equipment. Some day it is likely there will be a breathing apparatus during the day as well as the night and perhaps a feeding tube. The dance will continue to have new steps. And with graceful clumsiness (or is it clumsy grace?) we will keep rolling, one leg up and the other down, one leg up and the other down.

The race is two-thirds over. Someone is hollering at me to walk my bike to the place where I can park it for the next event. My legs are shaking and I can hardly breathe, but Jeff is there snapping pictures and saying, "I can't believe you biked all the way to the top! Most people were walking their bikes up that hill!"

I nod but I don't have enough breath to talk yet. I walk my bike on shaking legs back to its rack. As I walk, I look down at my legs. My knees are both throbbing and feel both too far away and too close.

I lean my bike in the parking spot, give the damp handlebars a reluctant, grateful little pat.

"Goodbye," I whisper, "gotta run."

part three

RUN

2 2 | *The Dreaded Run*

The running part of race day does not start well.

One astonishing thing about running in a tri, even a first one, even for a nonathlete such as myself, is the amount of gear you can collect. What goes on your feet? First no shoes (swim), then slip-on shoes (bike), then lace-up shoes (run).

Sliding out of my biking shoes and lacing up my running shoes turns out to be no problem. The rest of the transition is less smooth.

We had arranged that Jeff and Elijah would hand off my headphones at the transition. I had imagined grabbing them from their outstretched hands as I ran past, but when I get my shoes on and get to where they are, I don't see them holding anything.

"Where are the headphones?"

"Oh! I was so busy taking pictures, I forgot."

I suppress a sigh of irritation. The important thing now is not to deliver a short lecture on the Purpose of the Pit Crew; the important thing is to get going.

I dig around in the backpack, untangle the headphone wires and plug them in.

Eli and I had made a tentative plan that he would accompany me on the run, although he had not trained at all. I wasn't sure, at ten, he could go the distance. As soon as we are out of the bike corral, it becomes clear this will not work at all. My knee is doing its alternate throbbing and stabbing thing. I have to concentrate. Besides, I still have my bike helmet on. Oops.

We're just a few steps into the run, when I turn to Elijah, who, as we'd talked about, is right beside me.

"Honey, I think I have to do this myself. Besides, I need someone to take this helmet back to Dad. Can you do that?"

He looks confused and a little sad. More than most people, he hates deviating from a plan. But he does not argue. I feel a little sad, too. I've let him down now, but I know if we keep going, the let down will be bigger, because it will be three miles of me thinking about the next step, about my next step, not his. I do not have it in me to encourage him, because I will have to spend every ounce of energy I have encouraging myself.

And then I am alone, running. Well, walking, really, and then occasionally breaking into a half-hearted jog. I do not have a coach urging me on, like one couple I see ahead of me. Unlike the other runners who pass me in pairs or threes, I'm not with a friend. Except for Kelly Clarkson on my headphones assuring me that what doesn't kill me will make me stronger (my taste in workout music is absurdly terrible), I have no one. When my knee hurts, I stop, bend over and sob a little, keep going at a walk.

There are a few moments of human connection—a smile from one race volunteer, an encouraging word from another, a cup of water from a third. But mostly I limp along, trying to run until the pain in my knee overcomes me, and then walking for a while. Just like the bike portion, the run section of the race is a loop. I get to the turnaround and there's a little tent where people are handing out paper cups of water. I take one and slug it back, but it hardly makes a dent in my thirst. The sun is starting to feel hot on my head now. My little running skirt is slipping and I have to keep hiking it up.

I sing out loud and talk to myself and try to pretend that other racers aren't noticing this as they pass by. And there really are a lot of other racers passing by.

"One step, lightly, one step, lightly, one step, lightly," I chant under my breath, trying with my limping gait not to put too much weight on my knee.

After letting the others pass me back in the pool and coming in dead last for that leg of the race, I've vowed to embrace a more competitive spirit. I will remember that this is a race, and I will push ahead, try to be faster.

One step, lightly, one step, lightly, one step, lightly.

As we finally come back into the shade of the park where the race ends I, amazingly, pull up next to someone—another woman, a little older than me. I could pass her! Then I meet her eye.

"Hi! Great race!" she greets me.

"Yeah," I grunt.

"We're almost there, go ahead. You should go across the finish line first," she suggests.

"Oh, no, after you," I automatically and politely respond. She pulls ahead. Geez, even when I'm consciously trying I can't get ahead. I would kick myself but my knee hurts too much for kicking.

23 | *What You Want to See When You Want to See the Future*

I used to know a kid who could tell the future. He had a charming smile, and he was a little more earnest than the average fifteen-year-old guy. He had a trick that the rest of the youth group I led loved.

"Let me hold something of yours and I can see your future. I don't know how. It just kind of comes to me."

Looking back, I'm not sure now why I was leading the youth group. I was hardly more than a youth myself, definitely a very young early twenties. I don't remember now, if it even matters, why the kind Sunday school director or the young woman pastor for whom I had so much admiration thought that it would be a good idea for me to be the so-called leader of the group. I'm not even sure I knew what that meant, except that I was to teach a lesson every Sunday morning from the curriculum that was provided, which I did with the barest minimum of preparation, and even less understanding of what I was talking about. At least once, I was actually hung over. But even the nonhungover classes, the ones where I was just sleepy, I don't remember very well.

If you've spent any time at all in a middle-class church setting, then you know it is very common for the youth group to go on a mission trip. Mission trips please the adults in the church, who like to think of the young people working together building houses or feeding hungry people or (in our case) running a vacation Bible school in a housing project in some far-away locale. I don't know what the experience was like for the youth themselves—whether it was more memorable for them than our classes.

It certainly was more memorable for me, although my memories are a blur of images unrelated to the work we were supposed to be doing: Our newly pregnant pastor munching soda crackers from her sleeping bag on the borrowed church floor first thing every morning. The shiny black skin and chanting voices of the VBS kids singing on the bus "There WAS three jolLY fisherMAN fisherMAN fisherMAN . . ." The looks of dismay on the faces of members of the Sex Addicts Anonymous group when they realized they were accidentally scheduled in the same room as our group during one evening meal. And, most of all, the unexpected joy of being on the road, jammed into a big rented van on the long ride to the distant city. I loved the road trip—the windows open to the warm freeway air, Jars of Clay blasting '80s Christian rock from the van's stereo, and all of us hanging over the backs of seats and twisted as far as the confines of our seat belts would allow, clustered around the kid who could tell the future.

The girls held back giggles as he cupped their hair clips in his hand, closed his eyes, called for quiet, and then spoke slowly and deliberately, predicting careers as veterinarians, husbands with dark hair, many children. He really was so earnest. I guess it started as a game, but you could tell he took it seriously, this gift he had. And we all liked him, so we wanted to take it seriously, too.

When he held my ring, he hesitated, looked me right in the face, his eyes question marks, looked back down again at the token in his hand, took a breath, and met my eyes a second time and start talking. I don't remember now what he said. I only remember my own loud thoughts.

"He's making it up," I thought. The idea that he might be lying had not occurred to me with any of the others. With the others, I had not doubted that he, at least, believed everything he said.

"He sees something else, something he doesn't want to tell me." I thought. I wondered what he saw. At the time, I really wanted to know. At the time, I imagined he saw the Saturday night partying I thought I was hiding. Or maybe it was the girlfriend I was just beginning a relationship with, and was reluctant to introduce to the kind church people, welcoming as they were. Now, my mind flashed back to the boy in the van and I wondered if he saw this—me, trying to run but really limping forward on knees that hurt. I wondered if he saw this, or all the other limping I'd done in the years since he held my ring and looked me in the eye.

Most people run on damaged knees sometimes. Something will hold more hurt than they expect, require more courage than they think they have. What if, at the start of your life, a man held your life lightly as a trinket in the palm of his hand, gazed at you with sad and serious eyes, and told you, not a lie, but the truth of the hurt your life would hold? Would you be able to run forward if that were to happen? If you knew about the hurts in advance, would you prepare differently for the unexpected death, the pain of sudden disability, the broken relationships?

I suspect you would not.

It seems to me that the way through certain of life's pains is not to prepare for them, but to move through them one shaking step at a time, drawing on wells of courage and strength you did not, could not possibly know you had, until the moment when you need them.

I am talking now about the pains that come unexpectedly—fire, flood, fiasco. But there are also the pains you prepare for. Train for, even. I thought I had prepared for this day. I had certainly trained. But the hours, days, weeks of training did not really get me ready for this.

Of course, the sprint triathlon day is not all pain. At the end, I will say it was one of the most exhilarating days of my life. In all the pictures that Jeff takes of me that day, I am grinning ear to ear. Grinning as I thrash across the pool and back. Grinning as I creak my bike up that last impossible hill. Grinning even as I limp on one good knee over the finish line. And I use the word grin advisedly. Because a grin is a very particular kind of smile. It is unselfconscious, free of care, innocent even.

But I did not grin the whole time. This pain is not what the magazine articles promise ("3 Months to a More Fit You!"), not what my friends testify ("I never imagined it could feel this good to run!"), not what the inspirational quotation on the rec center wall shouts ("If you can dream it, you can be it!"). None of them say, "Your husband will take your picture and then you will run away around a corner and down a hill, through a tiny patch of woods, and then you will bend over and sob, 'I can't . . . I can't . . . I can't'."

It was race day. The day I had been preparing six months for, dreaming about for even longer. I weighed my options in that shady little spot in the woods.

Number one: Stop. Certainly not. There's my husband waiting at the finish line with a camera, for one thing. All the other people I have told that I am doing this, for another. And, for a third, a certain interior stubborn will, a will I have not known until now that I had, to finish this thing I've started.

Number two: Keep running. Whatever damage I have done is still being done with every step, but I really cannot imagine running any more. It's not just the hammer blow on my knee with every step. It's also the consideration of the future. More blows equal greater injury equals more pain, right?

Number three: Finish, but walk it. Embarrassing, but the only viable option. Everyone else is running. This is, after all, a race. A woman I know speeds past, her little running skirt already flapping like a victory flag in the wind. The important thing, I think, for the thousand-and-first time, is not to win. The important thing is to finish. I remember an interview with an athlete who came in last in a race.

"How do you feel about your time today?" the reporter smirked.

"I feel like I came in ahead of everyone who wasn't here today," the athlete replied. If I finish walking, I may come in last, but I will still come in ahead of everyone who wasn't there that day.

I start walking, one foot ahead of the other. The pain I feel when I walk, unlike when I run, is just bearable. I'm not one of these pain junkies, so it's surprising to me that I kept going that day. Not for me what Jane Fonda used to call "the burn" back in the '80s. Even watching other people's pain hurts. In college I saw "The Search for Signs of Intelligent Life in the Universe," Lily Tomlin's one woman show, and there was this scene where Tomlin held her hand above a lit candle, which made me squirm like I was the one getting scorched.

24 | *The Hospital Where It Began*

When I was two years old, I went into the hospital for heart surgery.

When my mom tells the story of that time she says, "You were such a weak little thing, always blue and out of breath. You couldn't even walk around the block without sitting on the curb to rest."

My dad says, "I watched a big orderly carry you away to the surgery, and when you came back you were under anesthesia, but your little back was still heaving, you were still sobbing even in your sleep."

A weak thing. Sobbing, even in my sleep. A helpless, frail victim. That was my story about who I was, not just when I was two but for a long time afterward. I'm not sure why that was the message I carried out of toddlerhood. Because I have other memories from that time, too, and they are luminous.

Catching fireflies and the gentle laughter of my parent's kind, bearded friends floating overheard. Feeling warm in the night air and knowing I was safe with my parent's smiling friends.

Mommy sliding a bright yellow shirt over my head, smiling with what looks like love and whispering, "This is your very own shirt, your birthday shirt."

The same feeling of safety and wonder as with the fireflies, only because of the ruffles, this time, and the cool, slippery polyester next to my skin. My soundtrack was Ella Jenkins's warm, unlovely voice telling me confidently that my street began at *my* house and it was a very special street.

Wonder. Joy. Safety.

Except for this.

Mom's voice, "I'm going to get some dinner. See that light in that building? I'll be right there. I'll be right back."

The hospital bed has high bars, less a crib than a prison. The rows of beds in the big ward stretch out behind me, one after another, and although I am facing away from them, I know they are there—the other sick kids. My hands wrap around the rail, my small teeth are sinking into the plastic edge and I'm sobbing as if my heart, as they say, would break. A nurse comes in behind me. I see her faint reflection in the window. The tall white hat, the scratchy dress, the round face. She clucks, "Heh! Why are you laughing?"

I was such a weak little thing. Sobbing alone, with no one even to witness. I was a victim, right?

In the middle of training for the tri, I suddenly got curious about what else had happened in that hospital, besides the crying at the window. I had often been curious before, but figured I didn't need more confirmation of what I already knew—that I was frail, weak, a sobber. I wondered now if that story, the story that had loomed so huge my whole life, was really all there was. I wondered if I could find out more.

I sent for my records. I was surprised at how simple that process was, and even more surprised that sending forty-year-old hospital records was a service provided free of charge. For a few days, I didn't open the envelope, just looked at it sitting heavily on the counter. When I started to read, I read the whole thick thing, from beginning to end, in one sitting.

To this day, I have a recurring nightmare. The scene changes, which is part of the horror of it, since I never know it is "the Dream" at first. The situation is always the same. In the nightmare, I'm looking for a place to go the bathroom. Sometimes there are rows of stalls, but they are all crowded and filthy, and I open the stall doors one after another in mounting frustration and disgust. Other times, the toilet is in the middle of a busy room or too tall or tippy to sit on.

I read the records of my trip to the hospital and for the first time traced this dream back to 1971, its meaning found in a nurse's notes from a few days after surgery:

> Sitting up in bed on
> bed pan Trying to void and have stool
> Parents here
> Had small stool with suppository

Nurse Johnson, wherever you are, you are a poet! The frustration, the horror, the tippy tallness, the lack of privacy processed in a lifetime of unsettling dreams are all conveyed so neatly in those twenty words.

I read other words, too. Some of them I couldn't understand. Some of them I read fast, skimming because I could not take the slightly smug, self-congratulatory tone of the surgeons.

I had always thought of myself, the child in the hospital, in the third person. "She was a weak little thing. She was sobbing, and no one came. She was crying even in her sleep."

Now, I read about myself in the third person view of other people. I read about cuttings open and stitchings-up and temperatures and bedpans and parent visits and "chatting pleasantly in her crib." Seen through the eyes of doctors and nurses scribbling notes at the end of a shift, I realized something new.

I was not a weak little thing. I was not a frail child, sobbing in her sleep. I was a survivor. I must have been strong, and, yes, brave, too. Inside that little girl was the woman I would grow up to be; a nonathlete who would talk in public and marry a seriously disabled man and train for a sprint triathlon.

I thought that the one snippet of crying at the window was all I carried into the rest of my life from that summer. Well, that, and a little stuffed tiger they let me choose out of a box of toys when I was discharged; a scar that starts just above my shoulder blade and ends just under my left breast; and a probably unwholesome fascination with books about unhealthy children (I can still quote the opening line of *The Secret Garden* from memory: "When Mary Lenox was sent to Misselthwaite Manor to live with her uncle, everyone agreed she was the most disagreeable looking child ever seen . . .").[8] But those souvenirs were not all. I carried courage, but I did not recognize it, and I called it fear. I carried resilience, and I didn't know what it was, so I called it weakness. I carried the open-heartedness that was my birthright, and that open-heartedness was not a vulnerability as I had always thought, but a strength.

"When a child is born," I used to explain, in the days before I read my records, "the bond between the heart and lungs should break. When it doesn't, they have to do surgery. That's what happened to me." Like most of what happened to me in the hospital, I had it all wrong.

"*Patent ductus arteriosus* (PDA)," says Mayoclinic.com, "is a persistent opening between two major blood vessels leading from the heart. This normal connection, called the *ductus arteriosus*, is a necessary part of the baby's circulatory system before birth. It usually closes shortly after the baby is born. However, in some individuals it remains open (patent)."

So, it turns out that the connection between heart and lungs didn't need to break as I always said. It needed help closing, to be healed. Three

---

8. Frances Hodgson Burnett, *The Secret Garden* (New York: Harper Classics,), 1.

thousand American babies are diagnosed with PDA every year. Some of the PDAs just grow together by themselves. Some are fixable with medicine, usually ibuprofen. Some few every year require surgery.

In his notes following the surgery in early September 1971, the chief resident in surgery, one Dr. Richard Dean, writes, "The patient tolerated the procedure quite well and did not have any difficulty during any aspect of the procedure."

A year later, I was seen again by a pediatric cardiologist with the musical name Dr. Ro Gowdamarajan. "Once the PDA is operated," he writes confidently if somewhat ungrammatically, "the child is essentially normal."

Most every study that I understand claims that there are no long-term consequences of PDA surgery. These experts and doctors—they hold my heart in one hand and look me in the eye. They speak earnestly and, unlike the boy in the van, they tell the truth as they know it. But what medical doctor can really see into the future, can really state with confidence the long-term consequence of being born, as I was, open-hearted?

TIIE BREATH JOURNALS: PART VIII

Dear Jesus,

"This is my body." These are the words you gave us to remember you by. We say "This is my body" and then we break bread and eat it. On a good day, the eating reminds us of forgiveness and community and the justice-table-where-all-will-have-plenty. It also reminds us of this. You came to us divine but human. You came to us in a body, a body just like ours.

Sometimes I think of you, of your body. I wonder what it was like for you. Did your ears ache too, when you got them out in the wind too much? Did you ever feel just a tiny bit queasy on one of those boats while you zipped back and forth across the Sea of Galilee? Did your knee creak when you stood all day telling us that the less blessed we thought we were, the more blessed we actually were? Scientists say you and your friends probably contended with discomforts I can't even actually imagine—bad teeth, lice, rickets.

And conversely, did you notice your body another way?

Did you rejoice in the strength it took to walk your disciples all the way from one end of the known freaking world to the other?

Did you take pleasure in reclining at the table, at the taste and texture of food in your mouth and in your belly?

Did you relish the coolness of water—the sea, the river, the cup—after a hot day in the desert?

Mostly I want to ask this:

Were you born open-hearted, too, Jesus?

25 | *The Outsider Complex*

The running eventually ends, as painful events do. At the end of the race, I spot Other Jennifer, my lane-mate from the pool event.

"Hey, we did it!" we say to each other. We meet each other's family and then drift apart.

I can't get too close because even now I have a familiar feeling. The feeling that all around me are the real athletes, that I am on the outside, looking in.

The feeling that any moment they are going to notice, turn their backs on me. It's like I can't believe that anyone would look at me in my tri suit, shake my hand, pat my shoulder, and say, "Good job!" and "You made it!" as if they really meant it. What my friend Rachel calls the Imposter Complex is as persistent as the throb in the knee. It's always there, but sometimes it stabs.

From my few years of school on Madeline Island, I remember wide, shiny wood floors, tall windows, and the intoxicating odor of the mimeograph closet. In those two rooms, we learned how to write haiku and cut pictures out of old *National Geographic* magazines and build an ethanol still. I remember watching Bob Barker on *The Price Is Right* every day instead of having recess. (Could that be real?) It was an eclectic education, useful in some ways, a little spotty in others. I never really did learn math, or the names of the countries of the world, or how to fit in to a tight-knit community that relied on and resented outsiders in equal measure.

Once, another child—some summer kid, I can't remember his name now—and I crouched after dark in the tall stand of cattails across the street from the parsonage. If we made scary noises as people walked by, we figured, they would think the little swamp was haunted. We waited awhile and when our first victim appeared we gave it everything we had. "Ooooo. Oooo." We moaned in as ghostly a way as we could. We earnestly believed we would really scare someone, but instead of running away, some guy strode right up to us. He parted the cattails and looked down at our reddening faces. We hadn't planned what to do in the event that one of our victims was actually brave enough to approach our lair. We had no idea what to do.

"What do you kids think you're doing?"

"Um. Being scary?"

"Well, you didn't scare me. Come on out of there."

He wasn't scared at all! In fact, he was laughing. That's how it was all the time. I was a part of that world, making earnest noises at it, but I was outside it too. My parents were DIYers before it was an acronym, vegetarians who ground their own grain with a hand grinder and fermented yogurt in little cups on the counter top. They were enthusiastic and tasty cooks, but the food we ate at home looked and tasted nothing like the rainbow-colored cereal and soft white bread my friends ate.

"Bulgur is vulgar!" I chanted the short poem I learned from another hippie's child.

"I can't have friends over here," I wailed, "You'll make them eat garbanzo beans! At a picnic table!"

It's true that we had a red wooden picnic table in the dining room, which I probably sort of liked, or else did not notice until some astonished visiting friend brought it to my attention. No one else had a picnic table, and I was envious of their wicker-seated chairs and the gleaming tops of their tables.

When I got older, with a family of my own, I felt a new kind of being an outsider. We were sick and we were outside looking in at healthy people.

It seems like we were all sick all spring and summer the year that Elijah turned three. We did other things, too, I guess. Jeff and I ate scrambled eggs and read *Game of Thrones* aloud to each other and tried to keep the Sharpie markers from the toddler. (That last one was to no avail, as we found later when we moved and slid the futon couch away from the wall to discover a couple years' worth of secret scribbles hidden behind it.)

We took photographs in our Easter clothes and hosted a baby shower in our rambly ranch house and made homemade Playdoh and threw it away when it got moldy.

Mostly, though, we were sick.

Eli's nose leaked all day, and he wheezed when he ran, which was pretty much all the time. I was in the middle of a headache that I was sure was going to be over any minute now, but that actually was going to last another couple of years.

And, Jeff, of course, couldn't walk or lift anything heavier than a cell phone or turn himself over in bed. That summer, he was another kind of sick, too—the hallucinating-from-high-fever, not-keeping-food-down, going-to-the-hospital kind of sick. Pneumonia.

Pneumonia is never a joke, but for someone like Jeff whose body is already weak, it can be a fatal danger. Without the strength to cough up the phlegm in the lungs, he could drown. Jeff's body fights off infection with a fever so high that he goes deep into some other land where I cannot join him, hallucinating flood and apocalypse, rolling his head from side to side.

We weren't living together the first time I was with Jeff when he hallucinated from a high fever. We were in the hot and heavy season of dating long distance—me in Minnesota and him a plane ride away in Seattle. He'd been sick for a little while, but I wasn't too worried because people get sick and then they, you know, get over it. But he kept getting sicker and sicker, his voice weaker and more distant over the phone.

I knew it was time to go when I told him I was starting to worry. I suggested that I come see him in Seattle and he responded dully, "Oh, I don't think it really matters."

Those were the ardent days when every phone call, every contact mattered very much. So I hung up and immediately figured out how to borrow money for a plane ticket west. I took a taxi from the airport and found him in his apartment barely able to lift his head from weakness and dehydration.

I don't know how I got him to the clinic, but it did not matter anyway, because when we got there, the tall skinny doctor refused to give him antibiotics. She did not literally shake her finger at him, but her voice dripped with disdain.

"Too many antibiotics are bad for you because if you take them every time you are sick, your body stops responding to them. They stop working," she explained as if we would have never heard this before. She told him to go home and take fluids and it would get better. The doctor could not understand. How could she understand? We were making earnest noises into the dark, and all that we were getting back was derisive laughter.

Finally, I bypassed the clinic and took Jeff directly to the emergency room. Seeing how dehydrated he was, they hooked him right up to an antibiotic drip.

Through the curtain, we could hear another guy moan and then gasp out, "Fell off a roof, I'm dying, man. Just give me something for the pain."

Then, the low, reassuring voice of the doctor, his words muffled but calm.

The doctor slid through the curtain to Jeff's bed, checked his watch. I remember, the way you remember small things at a time like that, that his watch seemed absurdly huge, like a sci-fi communication device on his wrist. He hefted the IV bag with the bewatched hand, touched Jeff's wrist with his other hand.

Jeff was already looking a lot better, an empty vessel filling with water.

Behind the curtain, the guy who had been gasping in pain a few minutes before was saying to his friends in a normal voice, "Yeah, sure, I can give you a ride home. Just wait, I'll be outta here soon."

The doctor rolled his eyes. We on the sick side of the curtain were suddenly the inside circle, the legitimate ones. It was the guy on the other side of the circle who wanted in, in to the land of the legitimately sick. Jeff caught the doctor's eye. The doc shook his head, let his breath out with a whoosh. And Jeff laughed. It was so great to hear him laughing, that I laughed too.

It was easy to laugh then, but those courtship days seemed so long ago. Now we had serious responsibilities—a marriage and a toddler and a house. This time we weren't laughing. The IV drip in the ER was not enough and Jeff was admitted. The sun was low in the sky when I took Elijah to see him. I'm not sure why I thought this was a good idea. Taking a three-year-old to a hospital room is just a big exercise in "no, don't touch that," so after a minute or two, I took him right out again.

The sun was setting and I thought about the pile of laundry to be folded in the quiet house. I couldn't face it just yet. Instead, we wandered over to a playground on the hospital grounds.

At three, Elijah was one of those kids who had not fully experienced a playground until he had touched everything.

During his reconnaissance of the little park, he found a small blue wooden maraca. After he waved it around a few times, Elijah grinned, and handed me the broken little wooden toy. I said thank you. The blue paint was cracked and I could just make out the faded words Puerta Vallarta in fancy script. I shook it. The maraca was cracked and the beads inside had fallen out. It no longer made a sound.

Elijah laughed and ran off again.

I was so tired. Tired from Jeff being sick, from having a headache, from chasing a toddler, from the laundry that waited. I was an empty gourd with no beads, cracked and discarded, trying to make noise into the darkness.

As I stood up, I intended to drop the maraca back on the bark chips, but I held onto it. It really was a tacky little thing. But in the rays of the setting sun, it shone, and I smiled a little as I called out Eli's name and held out my hand.

"Come on, honey. Time to go home."

In the long shadows of an empty playground at twilight, Elijah gave me something small and broken and precious. Something that looked without purpose or use to other people. Something that could bring joy only to those who loved each other enough to understand how lovely it was. Something that looked an awful lot like my life.

I strapped Elijah into his ridiculously complicated car seat. As we headed back to our house, Leonard Cohen growled from the car stereo his "Anthem." His, and my little family's.

Ring the bells that still can ring
Forget your perfect offering
There is a crack in everything
That's how the light gets in.[9]

---

9. Leonard Cohen, "Anthem," 1992–93, written by Shanna Crooks, Mike Strange, and Leonard Cohen, Copyright: Shanna Crooks Songs, Sony/ATV Songs LLC, Stranger Music Inc.

THE BREATH JOURNALS: PART IX

Winter, 2007:

At 4 A.M., I jumped out of bed because of the spiders, before I realized that a colony of spiders were not actually spinning their webs above the bed.

Then I fell back to sleep and dreamed that another pastor and I were in a high, sunny room and we were leading a prayer circle.

I asked Elijah if he'd like to lead us in prayer, so he took the bowl of water he was holding and dumped half of it over his own head, then walked around the circle, patting everyone's face with the water. Well, in the dream, it was so sweet that my heart wanted to burst, but then we had to mop up all that water.

I woke up thinking about baptisms and blessings and hearing the boy coughing and gasping a little.

Inhaler time. He fussed at first, but then the drugs kicked in and he got chatty and funny. Then he started to hum, but woozily, like a tiny drinker in the middle of a bender.

"What song is that, honey?"

"You know, Mommy." And then he sang muffled but clear through the mask.

Thank you, thank you,
Thank you in the morning,
thank you in the noon time.
Thank you, thank you,
Thank you when
the sun goes down . . ."

26 | *Getting on Like a House on Fire*

That year, the sick year, after Jeff got home from the hospital, it was Elijah's turn to go in for a while. Like his dad, sometimes his breath rested heavy in his lungs, could not get out. The hospital staff kept him in an extra day, not because he really needed it but so that I could rest, since I wasn't feeling that great either by then.

That was years ago and we made it through that sick year and the ones that followed. Everyone is much healthier now. Elijah outgrew, as they said he would, the breathing problems that engaged so much of our attention in his first four years. What he says he remembers about his hospital visits now is that he watched *Sponge Bob Squarepants* all night and whenever he pushed a red button a pretty nurse brought him chocolate pudding. Now we laugh and tell the story that he was so used to having what he wanted day and night that he lay in bed at eleven o'clock at night on his first night home from some hospital visit or other hollering, "I want a haaaammm sandwich! Bring me a ham sandwich!" Jeff's doing better, too. He started working at home, away from the plagues that run rampant on the city bus, in the crowded office. Life bumps along.

Still, you know those dreams where you are running and running but not moving? Sometimes, even though we are mostly healthier now and life is mostly easier now, it is like that. Half-running, half-walking, not making much progress in the last leg of the race feels like those days when my legs are moving and nothing is going forward. I felt like that one day last year when a crowd of firemen filled the house with their muscles and their device with the blurry screen for detecting fire through walls and their advice about wiring. But the house was not on fire.

I guess I should back up, but it's hard to know how far to go. Should I back up to yesterday, when I thought my biggest problem was making time for today's list? Or should I back up further than that? To when we bought the house, which is now not on fire? To the day when Jeff and I looked into each other's eyes and said, "I do" and "in sickness and in health" and "forever."

Let's back up to those words. Because when you say them, no matter who you are, there is no way to know what they will really come to mean. No one at all who has said them knows, I am certain of that. And if one is marrying into a disability, maybe that one knows less than most.

I certainly did not know. That when people look at us, they see one thing—a guy in a wheelchair. When people say, "I don't know how you do it, honey," they are talking about the big picture, the Wheelchair with a capital W. It's not the big Wheelchair with a capital W that is taxing, though. We've mostly got the big stuff figured out. It's the little stuff that slows us down.

Jeff works as a designer on computers all day. Images on computer screens are made up of tiny boxes called pixels, and the average screen has more than a million of them. When most of us look at a picture or a string of words on a computer screen, we see the big thing, a smooth whole. But not Jeff. He has been trained to see the pixels, tiny squares, and he knows that even one misplaced can cause the whole page to be askew.

Friday is my day off, a pixels kind of day, a day to attend to those small jaggy squares that, taken together, make the whole picture smoother. I was out buying stuff that would make it easier to deal with the stuff I already had. Home with the stuff to organize the stuff, I was moving stuff around.

Friday for Jeff is often a Rest Day. Jeff usually stays in bed the whole day. Sometimes I help him up so he can go to the bathroom and take a shower. If he's really tired, he skips even that. Today was a shower-rest-day, so among the stuff I was moving around was Jeff himself.

Usually, I smooth over the pixels of this part. There are so many steps to moving Jeff, and I would rather show you, if you ask, the whole smooth thing than the edges. So I usually say, "I helped Jeff get out of bed" and leave it at that. But here's what that means:

Like always, I rolled Jeff on his side in one, two, three pushes, trying to remember to move from the knees so I don't throw out my back. I wheeled the iBot out of the way and pulled a little footstool out from under the bed. I brought the shower chair (the one with the conveniently placed hole in the middle of the seat) in from the shower.

There were more small adjustments to make—a towel to arrange just so, sheets to pull back enough but not much, the hose from the breathing device Jeff wears in the night to be hung up. All this time, we were talking about small and familiar things, as we usually do. We talked about what we dreamed, perhaps, or our plans for the day as I pulled his naked legs by the knees and gently (careful of the feet! they are tender!) lowered his feet to the step stool. He was still lying on his side, but his feet were dangling over the edge of the bed.

With one arm, I slid into the curve between Jeff's shoulder and ear, and lifted him to a seated position, the crook of my elbow on his neck. For some reason I don't really understand, this is not uncomfortable for him. However, this is the scariest part for me because Jeff is not at all stable in this position—his toes barely brush the footstool and there's nothing on either side to hold him up.

The day before, I let go at the wrong time and he tipped slowly as a tree felled by loggers, cursing from fear and the anticipation of pulled muscles, back onto his pillow. He wasn't hurt after all, but I was nervous today, especially because he was talking about the new case he put on his phone since he figured it would not survive being dropped again.

"No talking about dropping right now, OK?" Then, remembering yesterday's fall and the power of suggestion, we were both trying not to giggle. Laughter makes him tippy.

I rested my hands on his shoulders and breathed in and then out. He nodded, ready for the next step, transferring via a cloth sling and a hydraulic lift to the shower chair. As soon as the sling was tucked in around his hips, I attached the loops to the lift and then I breathed easier because now he was securely held. I pushed on the handle, pumping it just like an old-fashioned water pump, which raised Jeff into the air. With some effort, because this was the only really hard physical part, I pushed the lift on its little wheels away from the bed and over the shower chair.

Like always, I made sure everything was just so, with the shower chair and the lift both in the exact right place. With one hand, I pushed Jeff's hip into position over the shower chair. With the other, I pushed the lever that releases the lift and he settled onto the shower bench. I pulled the sling out from under his thighs. I unlocked the wheels of the shower chair and pushed Jeff over the bathroom door lintel and onto the toilet, handing him his phone on the way so he could call me when he's ready to move to the sink to shave. He'd call me again when he was ready to get into the shower. Then I watched the clock, and after twenty minutes, I pulled back the shower curtain, handed him one towel while I dried off the hard-to-reach bits with another one, and pushed him out of the shower, back to the sink, and then back into bed, reversing all the business with the sling, the lift, and the careful-not-to-tip movements.

The whole project takes about an hour and a half. If it were a recipe, it would read "total time: 90 minutes; total hands-on-Jeff time: 20 minutes." I always think those extra seventy minutes will be good times to get things done. But really, I can never seem to get settled into anything.

After Jeff was done with what we call the Bathroom Steps and he'd been settled back in bed for a little while, I put the finishing touches on moving-stuff-around, which, as usual has taken much longer than I planned.

First, though, I was thinking about dinner. Truthfully? I'm nearly always thinking about dinner. This time I was both thinking and talking, wondering aloud to Jeff what I could make the leftovers do today when, with no fanfare or flare, the electricity in our room went out.

I think I forgot to say anything about Jeff's bed, which can raise and lower at head and feet, so he can move around when he's resting. He is too weak anymore to roll over himself, so the bed helps him move when he needs to at night. Now the bed was up both at head and feet, and with no electricity, he was stuck with his feet up in the air in an uncomfortable looking v-shape.

I was not too worried, thinking we probably blew a circuit with the space heater, but investigating, I opened the bathroom door and smelled melted metal. I didn't see any smoke or flames, but something was definitely on fire somewhere, which meant Jeff needed to get out of bed again. There's no way he was going to be able to stay in bed all that long in that position.

So we repeated the recipe, with the added wrinkle of negotiating the v-shape of the mattress. Instead of the shower chair, I settled him on his regular wheelchair, pulled a t-shirt over his head and wrestled him into his pants. Try having a friend pull your pants on while you are seated firmly but limply in a soft chair and you'll have some idea of what this entailed. Next socks, and then shoes. And then the shirt, and the thousand little adjustments the average person never considers in dressing. The bunched sleeve pulled even, the wrinkled pants around the knees smoothed.

The firemen (they were all men) arrived with their heat-seeking device and filled our house with advice and ideas but found no fire. Only a couple of hours later, when an electrician pal took down the light fixture in the bathroom, did we see the bundle of wires that had shorted out and melted, scorching the inside of our wall but never catching.

My mind is, as Anne Lamott writes somewhere, a dangerous neighborhood sometimes and not a good place to go wandering around alone. It took a huge effort not to walk down those dark streets. What if the bathroom had been on fire? How could I possibly have gotten Jeff up and out of bed on time? What if it had happened when I was gone and Jeff was alone in bed? What if, what if, what if . . . What If Avenue is the most dangerous street in all that dangerous neighborhood. I don't need a boy in a van to tell my future now. My mind takes me plenty of places all on its own.

People sometimes shake their heads and sigh and gaze at me and Jeff and say, "I don't know how you do it." But if you want to know the hard part of a disability like Jeff's, one that is progressive, this is what it is. It's both planning for, and continually backing away from, a disaster that never comes but is always lurking, just out of sight, just around the corner.

THE BREATH JOURNALS: PART X

Just breathe, people are always saying.

As if breathing is the simplest action there is.

As if there is nothing at all to opening your lungs fifteen times a minute to the elements, drawing those unseen molecules deep into your body, expelling them out again.

As if it is no big deal at all that we can do this without thinking about it, over and over. About 672,768,000 times in a lifetime. Six hundred seventy-two million, seven hundred and sixty-eight thousand times.

We should all be experts at breathing, with all that practice. But every day I wake up and have to learn how to do it again.

But first I have to remember that I don't know how to breathe, that I have to learn it.

It's this way with food. Sometimes I will wake up and have a green smoothie for breakfast, a salad and cup of lentil soup for lunch, an apple for a snack. Then on the way home, I will stop at McDonalds for a Big Mac and fries.

"I ate healthy already today," I explain to myself idling in the drive-through line, "I don't really have to do it again."

It's the same with exercise. Three days since the last time I exercised, my legs are stiff and cramping, something's starting to stiffen on the right side of my neck, and I find fault with everyone, starting with myself.

"Do I really have to do that again?" My inner child (the whiny annoying one, not the sweet one) asks. "I exercised already, like on Wednesday."

Sleep. "I already slept eight hours one night this week. I can catch five and half the next couple nights. Who will know?"

After a few days of this, I have to relearn what I know—how to do what we are supposed to come out of the womb knowing—how to eat, how to sleep, how to move my own body.

And how to breathe.

In the creation story that I know best, here's what happened. The Creator squatted in the dirt and, instead of making mud pies, made an Earth Creature. This Creature pleased the Creator, but at first it was limp and parched. Until the Creator put breath, air, into the lungs of the Creature, it could not live.

We are all Earth Creatures. But from the first moment, what made us live was the breath of the Creator, flowing in. And our breath responding, flowing out.

I have prayed so often by now. I've prayed written prayers—each word carefully crafted. I've prayed holding hands, linking a dying person and their most beloveds. I've prayed quietly and I've prayed out loud. I've prayed to bless meals and homes and babies. I've prayed in surprise, when something heavy dropped on my foot and I shouted "JESus Christ!" and then looked up and added "That was a prayer, not a swear."

But the simplest and the earliest is the best for me. I breathe in, I breathe out. As I breathe in, I say the name of God, remember that it was God who gave the first breath to the first creature, remember the astonishing truth that to breathe is my birthright, and also that my birthright has to be remembered every day—like moving my body, eating what nourishes me, sleeping enough.

Breathe in, God created you.
Breathe out, you are human.
Breathe in, you are human.
Breathe out, God created you.

27 | *Why I Can't Ever, Ever, Ever Get Sick. And What Happens When I Do*

Other caregivers tell me this, and it's true for me too. Our families are a house of cards. As much as we try to protect our loved ones, it's just as important to protect ourselves because so much depends on our strength and health. We feel that we are the one card that, if you pull it out, will collapse the whole structure. So we protect ourselves. We refuse to visit friends because we might bring home a cold; we do not join our family for the reunion this year because it's too far to travel. And we would never do something as ridiculous as train for a sprint triathlon because we might get hurt. I don't know what I might attempt if I were the only one who depended on the strength of my knees. I only know that I've attempted this relatively small athletic endeavor, and now my knee hurts and everyone in my family is affected.

To see if I can fix it, I'm meeting with a personal trainer at my local community center. I picked her because, based on her picture on the community center bulletin board, she seemed to be about my age. Also, her body looked normal, like a piece of challah, say, instead of like a piece of uncooked spaghetti.

Also, I've spied on her doing her personal trainer thing with an older guy at the neighborhood rec center. She sat near him while he sat on the edge of a bench and raised his knees one at a time in the air. He didn't even break a sweat, and they were both laughing. I figure if she can teach an octogenarian to raise his leg, she can help me do something about my knee.

Unfortunately, I do not get the sit-on-the-bench-leg-raise treatment. She has me on my hands and knees. She claims this is to strengthen my abdominal muscles, which, last time I checked, are nowhere near my knee. From her perch on the exercise ball, she instructs me.

"OK, squeeze your abs."

There is a pause while I try to locate my abs. What are they anyway? I squeeze something.

"I think I just did a kagel."

"Um, OK. Try this. Push like you're making a poo."

We both laugh out loud. Oh, there are the abs. Got it now.

It's so odd inhabiting this body and feeling like I am just getting to know it. But I know that uninhabiting my body all these decades has not really served me. It makes me sick in vague but uncomfortable and sometimes debilitating ways.

Elijah and Jeff got better that summer, but I kept being just a little bit sick. Finally, a few years later, I stopped being able to push through it and I sent this e-mail out to some friends.

Subject: Sick (and not the good kind)

Dear Friends,

I am writing to ask for your prayers, if that's your style, or your good thoughts if that is more your speed. Look out, a long and sort of intense e-mail is ahead, just to warn you. I'm not looking for advice or anything, but am hoping to have some witnesses to this moment in my life.

The last three weeks have been very difficult for me health-wise. I've been experiencing bouts of extreme dizziness, along with some bad headaches and even some nausea, along with exhaustion. At times this has been very debilitating, although I have kept working part of most days.

On Friday, I saw a neurologist, who ordered a whole bunch of tests. Not pregnant, btw, in case those symptoms are ringing any of your bells. This week I will have an MRI, which she said not to worry at all about, but is for the purpose of ruling out certain things (MS, tumors, strokes). She also drew blood to see if I have a vitamin D deficiency, and gave me an order to see a physical therapist to help with muscle tension in my neck and shoulders. She asked Jeff to watch me sleep some night, as her real suspicion is sleep apnea—this means an overnight sleep study is probably in my near future. She also gave me a prescription for an antidepressant.

None of this is easy, but the hardest to cope with is the depression. I have been fighting a depression diagnosis for a while, but (especially as the days get shorter) I can really tell that what I'm feeling is more than blue. It's easy to tell parishioners and loved ones that depression is an illness like any other, and that medicine really helps, but it's harder to tell myself. The internal chorus ("should have tried harder," "should have done better self-care sooner," "you just make yourself sick to get attention," and my old nemesis "lighten up") is singing pretty loud, and it makes it hard to pray, which makes me feel a little crazy. Jeff says that I am so good at hiding feeling depressed that it gets kind of stuck in my body and comes out in these dizzies, headaches, etc. He is right.

So today I went to get the meds, thinking, "Well, I can just have it in the house, I don't have to start *taking* it," and when I got to the Rite Aid, I started to cry when I heard Blood, Sweat & Tears on the Muzak:

And when I die
and when I'm gone

there'll be one child
born in this world
to carry on, to carry on.[10]

And I thought, "OK, it's time." I mean, that's a good song and everything, but I really don't need to start weeping whenever I run errands. If this medicine will help with that, then that's a good thing. (Didn't mean to freak you out with the dying thing, btw. I'm not at all suicidal. Which activates another unhelpful voice, "Well, you're not *really* depressed then.")

I have so little energy, but I really, really, really want to keep on working if I can, and with all the doctor's appointments that's about all I can do. I'm not very good at reaching out at the moment, and I'm not sure when I can be. But know you are in my grateful thoughts and (when I can manage them again) prayers.

When I read this, it actually seems like not that big a deal, but it took me the whole day to write it and get up the nerve to send it, so it must be some kind of a big deal to me.

Thanks for hearing this.

I am grateful,

Jennifer

In the end, it was not the MRI, CAT scan, or blood tests or medicine that ended the dizzy spell and also, incidentally, the headaches. In the end, what did the trick was a series of four easy movements called the Epley maneuver that I could do at home.

I sit with my head at forty-five degrees. I lay back, with my head still at the same angle. After a minute or so, I turn my head ninety degrees the other direction. I sit up. Then I do it on the other side. Then I stand up and walk into a day free of vertigo, nausea, headaches, exhaustion.

---

10. "And When I Die," written by Laura Nyro in 1964; first recorded by Peter, Paul, and Mary in 1966; popularized by the 1969 release by Blood, Sweat & Tears, www.songfacts.com.

The Epley maneuver is so ridiculously simple, yet the inventor, Dr. Epley, was such an uncharismatic guy that the idea almost died with him. In the 1970s and '80s, he would go to conferences with other doctors to present his idea that some dizziness was caused by little calcium crystals lodged in the circular part of the ear. He would suggest that those crystals could just be moved back to the inner ear where they belonged with a series of simple motions. Other physicians laughed, shouted invective, or walked out. After years of this, Epley's idea started to take root and now is a standard of care for what is called "benign vertigo."

Some people only have to have the Epley once and they are cured for life. Other people, like me, run in a near constant state of almost dizzy and need to perform it more often. The Epley is easy and not strenuous. It takes ten minutes, tops, and it causes immediate relief from symptoms that are completely abhorrent to most people, me included.

I'm on the way out the door, car keys in hand. Jeff, who has watched me nearly miss walking into the bathroom door that morning, calls after me, "Did you do your Epley?"

"Yes," I uncharacteristically lie. "Bye!'

In the car, I wonder why I lie about a little thing like this, when Jeff and I are so generally scrupulous about truth telling. I think about a friend of mine who's in recovery from alcohol addiction. In the early days, she explained to a sponsor at an AA meeting that she was getting stuck on her recovery every time she had to wash the car because she was used to washing the car while drinking a beer.

"What am I supposed to do?" my friend asked earnestly, expecting a wordy and complicated answer.

"Get a Snapple."

"What? I can't just drink a Snapple instead! This is a serious problem!" My friend protested.

"If my idea was hard, would you do it? Just get a Snapple."

This is a human problem, not a modern one. People told this story way before Snapple or cars or Dr. Epley. You can read this story as far back as the Bible.

Eons ago, there was this guy named Naaman, who had a pretty good life. He was an advisor to the king on the winning side of a war. The only thing that bugged him was this terrible rash he had all over his body.

A slave girl in his house, a prisoner of war from the enemy side, suggested he go visit the prophet from her side, the enemy side. It took some doing, but finally he heard from the great prophet himself. This was the message:

"Go and dip in the Jordan River seven times and you will be healed."

Now, the Jordan River is little, muddy, and unimpressive. Naaman was offended.

"Why should I bathe in this little stream? The rivers in my country are much grander than this one!"

He was about to storm off in a huff, when his advisers stopped him.

"Look, man, if it were difficult, wouldn't you do it? Just try."

He did and was healed.

I wonder if it were the seven times that kind of got to Naaman. After all, it's easy to be present and in the moment watching a beautiful sunset once a year at the beach, or releasing Eli as he takes his first steps, or even sitting with Jeff in the ER, because those things don't happen all that often. It's noticing the sunset from my own front porch, packing a lunch for Eli every freaking day, putting on Jeff's socks just so each morning—that's harder.

It's not this morning's Epley maneuver I dread; it's the Epley I'm going to have to do every day for the rest of my life. It's not this Saturday's Snapple that is hard for my friend to swallow; it's the Snapple she will drink every summer weekend, forever, that sticks in her craw.

Look, that's the thing about being in a body. It's so hard to limp along in this body knowing that I must keep limping—not just today and tomorrow and the next day—but every single day, day in and day out.

Once a year, when I gather with other women in the Women of the 14th Moon ceremony, we offer the youngest women drinks of both lemon water and honey water in order to prepare them for a life that is both bitter and sweet. At the end of the day, the oldest women are invited to share any wisdom they have with the younger ones.

Last year, a woman in red stood and began firmly, "I just want to tell you that perfection is . . ." she paused, looking for the exact right words and then went on ". . . an elusive goal."

A laugh of recognition rippled around the circle. It's elusive, but we keep running after it, all of us. I thought of that and of the drink we had given to the young women—bitter and sweet, sweet and bitter.

28 | *Floating Away and Coming Back to Earth*

Whenever we talked about our family friend Sister Rosemary, we always said,

"Rosemary is cool," although I'm not sure why, because really she was the opposite of cool. She was sensible and kind and her eyes crinkled with she laughed. When I was thirteen, I went to spend the night at her apartment. My brothers and I tended to run in a pack, so I'm not sure why it was just me in Sister Rosemary's simple apartment. Before we went to sleep, we sat on her hard little couch and held hands to pray. Or rather, Rosemary prayed and I sat there feeling self-conscious.

"Thank you, Jennifer," she said after she was done speaking. "You have a beautiful spirit and it's wonderful to pray with you." Then we went to sleep.

I hadn't prayed at all. I thought that made me a faker and probably a bad person. I hadn't yet learned what Sister Rosemary knew, that none of us are all one thing and that inside the awkward, anxious teenager on her couch was also a beautiful soul, someone with whom it was a joy to pray.

I'm not a young woman anymore. Most of the time when I taste the bitter I remember that life also holds sweet, and when I taste the sweet, I remember how many taste the bitter.

You know that when I was a baby, I was in the hospital for a while. Besides the crying and the little stuffed tiger, one of my other memories of the hospital is this: I am looking down on a woman sitting next to a crib. In the crib is a child. I look closer. The child is me. The woman is my mother.

Now I'm forty-three years old. With the training for this tri, I feel like I'm moving into this body for the first time since I'd gone floating out of it as a baby in the hospital. It seems weird to me that I have not really lived in my body until now. Where have I been? For most of my life, I have worn baggy turtleneck shirts, long skirts, heavy shoes. Really, it was more like armor than clothing. I was like a floating head with no body at all underneath.

My parents were not this way. They were aggressively casual about their bodies. In 1978, my mom gave birth to one of my brothers in the living room on a red bean-bag chair while my cat brought her new-born kittens one at a time and placed them around her like an offering.

A few years later, I was out of the house one summer afternoon. For some reason I wasn't with Sarah and Cathy, to whom I'd cleaved with fierce devotion after all the solitary traumas of summer camp. My friends rang the doorbell. My mom was in the bath and she couldn't find her towel, so she just answered the door as she was, dripping wet and naked as the day she gave birth to Noah on the living room floor.

"Oh, girls!" she cried, a big smile on her face, "I'm so glad it's you!"

I wonder if it's related that my parents were so casual both about their bodies and their houses. We changed houses every year or so until I was twelve. It seemed like we were always either unpacking or packing, getting ready to move or moving in.

For the first three decades of my life, there was almost nothing I loved more than moving into a new house. Unlike most people, I guess, I loved all of it. I loved packing and culling possessions, cleaning out all the dusty corners. I loved the fresh start in a new place, deciding where to arrange the furniture, hang the pictures, putting the vegetable peeler where I could find it the first time I needed it. The rewards are immediate. And I moved so often, I did not spend too much time thinking about or caring for the houses I lived in. If a hinge got busted there, or a wall scratched here, who cared? There would always be another one in the next house.

Moving into my body for the first time in my life does not have the same immediate pleasure. Instead, muscles spasm unexpectedly. Legs cramp at night. My head hurts. I have to really understand what I'm eating for every single meal.

When I was a child and something scary and incomprehensible happened to me, it served me well to float up and out of my body, to escape from pain and confusion. As I got older, that coping technique did not serve me any better than training wheels or potty chairs or bib overalls, but I kept using it because it was all I knew. I did not know that floating protected me from the amazing pleasures of my body too. Wind in my hair, the particular way my arm pulls through water, the feeling of new muscle where there was none before—this is what I was protecting myself from, I realize as I train day by day.

When I feel the twinge of knees, the spasm of muscles, the temptation is there to float up and away, to move out. Time now to dust out the corners, unpack the boxes and hang the pictures. Time to drink both the bitter and the sweet. Time to move into my body for good.

29 | *There's No Medal for Fifth from the End*

At birth, I was—we all were—handed this body with all its aches and pleasures. I don't know how you responded. Lately I'm feeling like the Holy One gave me a life and said, "This is your body," and then I stuck my fingers in my ears and yelled.

"Lalalalalalala!"

It wasn't that way every single minute. Every now and then, I pulled my fingers out of my ears, paid attention to the words, and felt what it meant to really be, and be in, this body I'd been given.

When I was a young adult, working my first real job at a school in northern Minnesota, I would sometimes meet another teacher at this one lighted ski track in the evenings. She would come slushing up through the snow and throw open the door of her rusty old station wagon, "Do You Hear What I Hear?" blasting from her AM radio. We'd click our ski shoes into their toe holds and take off, the other teacher zooming quickly and easily far ahead. In those moments, I would feel what I imagined a real athlete felt like. After the rush of getting ready, it was totally quiet in the woods, except for my own breathing. I took some steep climbs up, breathing hard, and then some exhilarating shout-out-loud sweeps down. Sometimes I would fall but the snow on the edge was soft and caught me easily. The trail was lighted, but not continuously, so between pools of light, the stars shown down clear and cold. In my mind, I would narrate my two loops around the track as if I were running a race, as if I were an athlete who could compete and win. Push, pull, glide. Push, pull, glide. Before I could swim, before I could ride, before I could even run, just a little, I thought for those few minutes that I knew exactly what being an athlete felt like. Now I'm not so sure.

A year after the triathlon, I went on a sabbatical for a summer. Before I learned to swim, I had asked a lifeguard if he could teach a nonswimmer who was afraid to put her face in the water to surf. He said no. During that summer sabbatical I learned I could not only swim, I could surf!

Borrowing a joke from a friend, I nicknamed the summer away "Surfbatical," and started a little blog about it. My brother Mark works sometimes for Google and called me, crowing with as much delight as if it had been his idea, "You own "surfbatical"! Did you know that?" Evidently no one else has coined this weird little word before.

Well, maybe I can make up words better than I can surf. And although I am still not exactly at home in your gymnasium, gym rat, at least I can go there when I feel like it. I still don't call myself an athlete. I think that's because an athlete is really a competitor, and as I had come to see even when I tried to compete, I was kind of ridiculously bad at it.

Whether athletes are competing against other athletes for a medal or not, they are still going for the prize.

"Surfing! Did you love it? Are you good at it now?" Mark called and enthused after my summer away. I did not get the prize in surfing. Not even the prize of being able to answer his question with a "yes." Because no, I am not any good at surfing now. Even if athletes are not competing against someone else, they are competing against themselves, their best previous record.

In my church, we practice two sacraments—baptism and communion. We say that these two practices are a visible sign of an invisible grace. At these times, we say, God's love breaks through that veil that so often separates us from our knowledge of the work of the Divine. When I serve communion, I hold up bread, I break it, and I say Jesus' words, "This is my body." I have spoken these words so many times without realizing that Jesus is giving me a sacrament, too.

It is one of the great joys of being a pastor that I am able to offer the sacraments, but every once in a great while, I get to be someplace where they are offered by someone else, where I get to receive them. On one of those times, I heard Christ saying new words, a new sacrament, not just for me, but for Jeff, for everyone. "This is *your* body. Sometimes it will hurt, sometimes there will be pleasure, sometimes it will just be a grind. But it is a sacrament, making visible a grace that has been invisible all this time. It's no accident," the Voice continues, "that grace is both the word for the way God works in the world and the way our bodies move with the most ease and beauty. This is your body."

True, I cannot be an athlete. I never did tell you how I placed in that race, did I? Well I came in fifth. Fifth from the end, that is. That's right, on that day there were just four people who sucked more at the tri than I did. Someone held up an empty box. "Sorry, we're all out of medals." I felt like I should care about that, but I didn't. I just don't care about competing enough, either with myself or with other people. Even when I'm in an actual race, as I found out in the triathlon, I can't muster up enough of the . . . the . . . whatever-it-is that pushes other people to pull ahead.

So maybe I can be, I don't know, a sacralete instead. It's not a competition, but I can just keep moving, because the more I move my body, the more God's invisible grace is made visible.

It's true that the McMinnville Oregon Parks and Rec Sprint Triathlon is a pretty low-key tri, and there is just a small knot of people at the end, but I don't see Jeff and Elijah right away. I think of all the races at which I have cheered on family, friends. I raise my hands, inviting applause and a few people laugh and clap.

And then, I am across the finish line, raising my arms and shouting.

Jeff and Eli find me and they are patting me, saying encouraging things, showing me where I can go to look up my time and asking me if I want a slice of orange.

My knee is throbbing but I feel ecstatic. Sometimes things will just hurt, but that doesn't have to stop me and it doesn't this time.

part four

BREATHE

THE BREATH JOURNALS: PART XI

I will go to Hawaii, where people really do say "Aloha" when they greet you.

A beautiful young woman will earnestly explain to me that "aloha" means "I see and honor the Light in you"

Somewhere else I will read that "aloha" comes from the ancient Hawaiian word for breath, as in:

"You Are As Vital, As Precious As My Very Breath."

We can't really know where this word comes from, so there's no way to know if either of these explanations are factual.

But both are true.

We have plenty of facts

> *and all the information on the Internet, considered as electrons,*
> *weighs a millionth of an ounce,*
> *less than a fingerprint, a tear . . .*[11]

I learn another word when I'm in Hawaii. "Haole" means whitey, foreigner. In the manner of ethnic nicknames, it sometimes is affectionate and kidding, sometimes hateful and venomous.

Somewhere I read that "haole" means "people who don't know their own stories." This is because the first white people could not recite the story of their ancestors, all the way back to creation, as the Hawaiians could.

Somewhere else I read that the word comes from "ha-ole," meaning "no breath." This is because the foreigners did not greet one another nose to nose.

---

11. From James Richardson's poem "Are We Alone? Or Physics You Can Do at Home" in *By the Numbers* (Port Townsend, WA: Copper Canyon Press, 2010), 63.

Or maybe it is because the first missionaries did not breathe three times before prayer, as was customary on the islands before then.

Neither of these anecdotes are probably factual either.

But they are true.

"But this, too, is true," writes Tim O'Brien. "Stories can save us."[12]

If I know what my stories are, will I keep breathing? Will I stay alive?

The only way to find out, I guess, is just to tell them. Tell my stories. All of them. And then see what happens.

CODA | *Swim, Ride, Run, Breathe, and . . . Surf. Or, On Living Exuberantly*

I joke with my friends at home about the surf instructors I'm going to meet in Hawaii because their real names are Summer and Eduardo.

They are both exactly like you'd think from their names. Summer is lean and tan and friendly and very beautiful. She has that long blonde hair that you'd think would make her a native of Malibu, although it turns out she is from Texas. Eduardo is Brazilian—wiry and gorgeous and confident. When he takes me surfing the first time and I want to cry from how hard it is, he zooms past me, standing on his head until I laugh and get back on my board.

---

12. Tim O'Brien, *The Things They Carried* (New York: Houghton Mifflin, 1990), 225.

"I'll teach you that in tomorrow's lesson," he promises.

The next morning I meet Summer for yoga on a patch of damp grass looking out toward the Pacific Ocean. She balls up her tiny fist and gently whacks her pubic bone.

"You need to get your strength from here," Summer says.

That day, the second surfing lesson is harder than the first.

I am stiff and sore from yesterday's repeated fallings and gettings-back-up and my knee was doing that throbbing/stabbing thing that I had finally learned is something simple according to a physical therapist called a "lack of engagement of the quads." "Your quads are not used to being used," he adds. "You have to remind them to engage."

As Eduardo pulls the surfboards out of a truck parked in the beach lot, I stretch, lean down to touch my toes, and make eye contact with my disengaged quads.

"Engage, OK?" I whisper to the spot where I think my quads are. I don't hear anything in response but I hope I've communicated.

I push the surfboard out to the break, get on it, fall down, get on it, fall down, while Eduardo offers encouragement and instruction and the occasional high five.

"You can do this," he says, "You just have to trust your body."

"Yeah, you make that sound so easy," I complain, then shoot off the wave, crash into the water again.

I do not trust my body. Certainly not since middle school when I shot up six inches or so, got a permanent that gave me Van Halen groupie hair, started menstruating, wet my pants during a play, and started getting crushes on boys that made me blush and grin so uncontrollably that this seventh grade guy called Curtis nicknamed me Chipmunk Cheeks.

As I'm paddling the board back to the break, I carry on a conversation in my head:

"I mean, honestly, is this a body you would call trustworthy? Sometimes when I'm tired my body won't sleep. Sometimes I'm so dizzy I have to lie down. My left knee hurts. My right knee strains to bend. My ears don't hear; they get achy in even the slightest wind. My left arm goes numb and my neck hurts from being on the computer or driving a car. My bladder lets loose at inconvenient times. I get anxious and suddenly I can't breathe. My skin does not tan in bright sun or even burn—it rashes. Speaking of rashes, did you know if I eat chocolate I get a rash? Also a headache and heart palpitations."

Tired of the conversation in my head, I try talking out loud. "Trust has to be earned," I mutter to my knees, my bladder, my left arm, my head, the sunburn on the back of my legs.

When I get back on the board, Eduardo suggests I think of yoga, imagine warrior pose. Both feet firmly planted, one knee straight and one bent, arms straight out. My favorite pose! I can do that.

"Warrior, Warrior, Warrior," I chant as I turned the board around, get ready to try again.

The water is warm, saline, green. I grew up on the shores of Lake Superior, and her cold waters felt alive to me. I had a friend named Karie who came from the East Coast and was used to the ocean. She complained about the Lake.

"That's not really water, that's not living, it's dead."

When I told another friend from my hometown about Karie's complaint, she nodded thoughtfully.

"I can see what she means. To me, the ocean seems alarmingly fecund."

Alarmingly fecund. So alive, so ready to give birth, so bursting forth with living things that it startles.

I pop up to my knees, still chanting, "Warrior, Warrior . . ."

Under there, the ocean is alive, is alive, is alive. And up here, I am alive too. What if I stopped haranguing my body, stopped shaming it for all the ways I could not trust it, and started trusting it?

After a while, Eduardo gives me a break from surfing because, really, I am a terrible surfer, and we oar a paddle board out beyond the wave breaks. Maybe ten feet from the bow of the board (does a paddle board have a bow?) a Something surfaces, a sleek body that rises and just as quickly is gone again.

Eduardo: "Whoa, did you see that? What was that?"

Me: (thinking) *How am I supposed to know? Aren't you the one who's FROM here?* (And saying) "I don't know, but if it was a shark, I'm going to freak out."

Eduardo: "I think freaking out is the worst thing you can do, right?"

Me: (Breathing, breathing, breathing. And getting calmer.)

Eduardo: (reverently) "It's a turtle. Look."

And behind us now and off to the other side, a turtle's head bigger than my fist peeks up.

I am not breathing now. I am holding my breath, but in a good way, in the way of someone in the presence of the Holy. There's a creation story that says that the earth was created when the Turtle went down to the bottom of the ocean and came back up covered with mud and growing things. And that's how everything was born. I am not going to die, not this time. I am going to be born.

There's life there, in the cloudy salt water, stirred up by the feet and falls of a hundred novice surfers here on the easy beach in the early morning. And there's life inside me, too.

At home, I often dash to my car each morning without stopping even for as long as a breath to see the spindly lavender growing in my front yard, the robin pulling worms out of the wet leaves or the way the clouds each move at their own speed like people moving along a city street.

In the same exact way, I ignore my body, shove food into it without paying attention to what is being shoved, refuse to exercise, sleep at odd hours or not at all.

Later, I get back on the surfboard, stand and chant, and then ride. My body, with all its failings, is trustworthy after all. Not only trustworthy, the ocean reminds me. Not only useful or even beautiful, but sacred, a sacrament, a visible sign of God's invisible grace and worthy of love and respect and honor.

It may seem ridiculous to compare my own little body to the whole big world. But they are more connected than I usually believe. If all of creation is sacred, that includes the turtles that surface at just the right time, the dolphins that jump around our boat in musical pods, the roaches in my rented room that no one can seem to get rid of, and my own untrustworthy, trustworthy body. I am no athlete, but it doesn't matter. I'm a sacralete.

I tap my fist on my pubic bone and think, "My power comes from here." I stand and then the surfboard is moving. I'm moving along with it for a few seconds of pure unbelieving exhilaration. And then, instead of falling, that time at least, I remember to crouch back down to grab the edges of the surf board, to sit up and pump my fist in the air, and then to lay back into the ocean's milky embrace.

I paddle back out to the break another time. Every moment of my life—in hospitals and summer camps and van rides and churches; all the frustration and love of marriage and parenthood; all those hours in pools and on bikes and lacing up running shoes—made it possible to be here now. I roll on my back into the alarmingly, astonishingly fecund water and look up at the sky and shout, getting salt water in my mouth but not caring at all, "Thank you! Thank you for all of it!"

And then I stand and—terribly and exuberantly—surf again.